Hurt

By

My Destiny

Marquentin J. Holland

IN LOVING MEMORY OF MY PARENTS

George Holland, Jr. and Valerie L. Holland

The Missing Peace

I knew one day you would depart from us,
but I didn't think it would be so soon
I was left staring at an empty room
I shed many tears and had even more fears
Anger, depression, and lived in solitude
I recalled the good times I sang your favorite songs
In life, I loved you dearly; in death, I do the same
It broke my heart to lose you and cost me overwhelming pain

You did not leave this earth alone
A part of me went with you the day God called you home
You left me beautiful memories; your love is still my guide
and though we miss you dearly, you're always at my side
Life is but a blur, a difficult puzzle with missing pieces
You had to be returned to your Maker
You were here just for a short lease
But my heart aches for you; you are my missing peace

DEDICATION

For the gift that you are and the light you have been in my life, for being a partner, and for being a friend. For being an encourager, for being a pain, for making me smile, and for driving me insane.

For sustenance and unconditional love, for lifting me in prayer, but most importantly, for always being there for me. I say thank you; for truly you are my good thing. You are much more than a wife; you're my best friend. I am thankful to have a partner like you in my life. I cherish everyone moment I have with you.

To my wife, Jasmine, I love you immensely, and I dedicate my first book to you.

Table of Contents

Acknowledgments

Writing a book is more daunting than I thought and more rewarding than I could have ever imagined. First, I give honor and praise to my Lord and Savior, Jesus Christ. Without him, I am nothing, but with him, I can do all things. Also, I would like to give special thanks to my best friend and wife, Jasmine. She has been there since the very beginning and supported me enormously throughout the process of writing this book—reading rough drafts, editing, and giving necessary feedback. She is my love and inspiration behind writing this book.

I would like to acknowledge my family for their love, care, and support. Thanks to my brother, Brandon, for always being the person I can turn to during hard times and for leading the way by publishing his first book two years ago. Your strength encourages me. Also, I am always appreciative of Uncle Ray and Aunt Gina; the things they do for me are immeasurable. They have played the role of parents in my life, and I am forever grateful for their support. To my grandmother, uncles, aunts, cousins, and in-laws, I say thank you, and I love you all.

I would also like to give a special thanks to Darius Owens. He shared his story and encouraged me a lot. Thanks to Alecia Truss for sharing her story as well. Thanks to Pastor Ted and Monique Chatman and my entire World

Changers church family for their unconditional love and support. I also want to give special thanks to Bishop Robert Lewis, Minister Robert Pitts, and Abundant Life Fellowship Church in Montgomery for their continuous thoughts, prayers, and encouragement. I would like to acknowledge my 7 Line brothers (8 Faithful Soldiers of the Bloodied but Unbowed) Omega Psi Phi Fraternity Incorporated, Theta Tau Chapter, Spring 22. I would like to thank everyone who has played any part in my life, whether significant or not. I appreciate you all.

Having an idea and turning it into a book is as hard as it sounds. Writing about true events has been a surreal process. I found it to be not only difficult but therapeutic, both internally challenging yet rewarding. To anyone who had a hand in publishing, marketing, and supporting me in general, thank you. I'm forever indebted to all those who played a major part in the completion of my first book. As I wrote my own story, I found these pages filled with tears. I pray that my testimony will help someone else. God bless you all.

Marquentin J. Holland

Foreword

If life is but a vapor, you had better enjoy it while you have it. If life is but a vapor, every day, hour, minute, and second should be lived with purpose, fulfillment, and intentionality. And if tomorrow is not promised—if we don't know what the future holds—shouldn't we live our best life today? But wait. What if you are longing for peace, happiness, and everything wonderful, but it seems too far out of reach? It seems as if life's circumstances (trauma, calamity, death, sickness, and a whole list of factors that are outside of your circle of influence) put you at a disadvantage from reaching your happy place. Or do they? What if your setbacks were setups for comebacks?

If you're like me, you are part of a mega-group that I like to call "Silent Sufferers." We function almost too well, no matter the adversity. We are leaders, educators, managers, creators, and innovators. When we dress, we grab our smile and put it on as if it were a part of our wardrobe. Our social media pages look like pictures of perfection. We mask our inner fears, pain, and disappointments with an artificial personality of "everything is perfect." Silent sufferers don't particularly like the attention that feels like pity. Furthermore, trying to explain the complexity of our pain doesn't seem worth it. Therefore, we switch on our smiles and laughter for our public profiles and change our settings to private when we cry, when we hate ourselves, when we feel hopeless, and when we lose. However, there is hope. Marquentin J. Holland takes you on a journey through his life and the lives of others who understand the depths of despair. I encourage you to read every page and every story. You will certainly find hope in knowing that you are not alone, and if so many others have learned how to overcome, you too can become an overcomer. You'll find that you no longer have to "BE" anything but authentically you. You'll learn to own your past, your hurt, your abuse, and your pain. You'll learn to accept all of you: the good, the bad, and the ugly. But don't take my word for it; turn the page.

Lady Monique Chatman

World Changers Empowerment Center
Anniston, Alabama

Preface

A clinical psychologist, Christina G. Hibbert, PsyD, knows a lot about tough times. Her youngest sister died from cancer at eight years old. In 2007, another sister and her brother-in-law died within two months of each other. At the time, Hibbert was just several weeks away from giving birth to her fourth child. Almost overnight, she inherited her nephews and became a mom of six. "I have been a daughter in grief, a sister in grief, and a mother raising kids in grief. I know it is not easy." **(Tartakovsky)** Maybe you're going through a similar experience or are grieving another kind of loss: a romantic relationship, a friendship, a job, or a house. Maybe there's a completely different stressor in your life. Whether it be sickness, pain, taking care of ailing parents, trouble finding a mate, financial hardships, depression, anxiety, bullying…whatever you are struggling with, just remember, as the poet Edgar Albert Guest wrote:

"Even hope may seem but futile,
When with troubles you're beset,
But remember you are facing
Just what other men have met."

In this life, we all go through some type of trouble. Trouble is inevitable, and we will all encounter some type of hardship at some point in our lives. The Bible articulates this in Job 14:1, "Man that is born of a woman is of few days, and full of trouble." Since we all fit that description whether we are male or female, we surely are not excluded from trouble. Whether you are a Christian, Buddhist, Muslim, Catholic, Jew, Baptist, atheist, or you believe only in science, the avoidance of trouble is impossible. There is no way you can live in this world and not deal with some type of heartache or pain. One of the Christian fairy tales that should be silenced is the belief that when you follow Jesus Christ, all of your problems are eliminated. NEWS FLASH: they aren't. Your soul is indeed safe from the condemnation of hell, but then comes a whole new set of problems that you didn't face as an unbeliever. Christians who claim to be without problems are either not telling the truth or are living in a make-believe world. My childhood pastor Dr. Leonard L. Jacobs, use to say, "In this life, you're either in a storm, coming out of a storm, or heading into one."

Just as surely as you are reading the words on these pages, you can believe, that troubles will arise at some point in your life. While I am a Christian and a believer in the Lord Jesus Christ, I am not writing this book as a Christian. I am simply writing this from the perspective of someone who has had trouble in this life. As we journey throughout this book, you will read different stories about trials and tribulations that some of my friends, family, and I have gone through—the many hardships that were faced in our lives and some of the ways we overcame them.

Smiling but Scarred

Many people think they know what it's like dealing with depression; some think it isn't real, some think it can be prayed away, and others think it will just somehow disappear by carrying on with their daily routines. However, that was not how it worked for me. In my ignorance, I did not understand how depression had deeply affected my life. I covered my pain with jokes and laughter. I was truly smiling, but scarred.

I was 14 years old when I lost my mother to what many would term a "freak accident." She was a full-figured woman, and this eventually created some health issues for her. At the young age of 34, she was set to begin dialysis. Her kidneys failed, and she needed a transplant. Moreover, she dealt with self-esteem issues, which encouraged her to attempt a gastric bypass surgery in order to lose weight. It was after this surgery that I lost my mother. The surgery appeared successful, and everything seemed to be okay until...it wasn't.

I had never seen my father cry until the demise of my mother. His tears were so real, and you could see that he was deeply pained. My mom was gone. They had been married for over a decade and a half, and she was his best friend. They were in love from a very young age, although he was about six years older than her. He was 21 years old when he met her, and she was 15. At the time, their relationship may have seemed odd, but they were so in love with each other. I was asleep the night Mom passed on, so I came to know about it the following morning. It was my dad who woke me up, crying as he gave me the biggest hug anyone had ever given me before. Having an old-school mentality, he wasn't quite an affectionate person. He, however, showed he loved us by being there to take care of his family every day. He was a provider, making sure we never went hungry or longed for anything. Even when we were disciplined, we knew it was done in love. I don't recall him ever actually saying, "I love you," but I knew he did because his presence was always felt. His presence spoke all that his mouth didn't. Now, my father was doing something out of the norm, hugging me and crying at the same time.

In my heart, I knew life would never be the same. As I reflect on that unforgettable day, my eyes still fill with tears. Truth be told, I wrote most of the other stories in this book before writing my own because I did not want to deal with the pain; the pain that came from remembering this time in my life. I can vividly recall that day. I asked my dad why he was crying, and he told me my mother hadn't made it. I remember the deep sadness that consumed me at that moment. My dad and I sat and cried for a while, and then I got up to make my bed as I normally would. I remember him telling me not to worry about it, but I went ahead and did it anyway. I then took a shower and got dressed. It was what I was accustomed to doing every morning. This was the way I pretended everything was normal, even if only for a moment. I listened to my dad's phone calls as they continued to come in, and I could hear my mom's friends and some family members crying. I then began sobbing again. I asked myself why this was happening. This wasn't fair! My mom was only 36 years old. She wasn't going to be there to cook for me or ask me to go to bed. She wasn't going to be there when I turned 18 and moved off to college. It was so painful, and the pain overwhelmed me. My parents had always told me to be strong because it wasn't a good thing for a man to show emotions. Dad forbade us from expressing our emotions; he just wanted us to be as tough as he thought all men should. That was the way he was raised, and it was the way he knew best to raise us. He taught us to fight through adversity and conquer pain. So, I just sat there with the hurt and pain, trying to be this man that my dad had brought me up to be, even though I literally was a child. I remember wishing desperately that the pain would just disappear and I would feel better again.

Thursday was the day my mother passed on. The next day, I went to my football game, like usual, as if nothing had happened. This was me, yet again, trying to be the strong man my dad had always taught me to be. Just a week prior, I was a normal kid, playing in the game, but this time, I just sat and watched others play. It was my freshman year in high school. I remember how all my friends came and hugged me afterward, telling me they were praying for me and that I should remain strong. I did remain strong outwardly. I didn't cry. After all the encouragement from my friends, I found a little strength.

For the most part, everything seemed fine in our family. We were handling it well, or so it seemed. What I didn't know at the time was that my dad was dealing with depression. I was only 14 years old then and completely unaware of the depths of his despair. Presently, I am 34 years old, and I am certain he was clinically depressed back then. He never went to see any doctors, so he was never diagnosed. Eventually, he started acting out of character, and that wasn't typical of him. He wasn't eating anymore, and he would always make excuses for that. My mom taught us how to cook while growing up, so I made sure to prepare breakfast and dinner for him every day. I knew that he definitely would not do it himself. I just wanted to help out. He was my father, after all. He was used to my mom taking care of him and taking care of the house as well. I tried my best to do the same so that he would have nothing to worry about, but I just couldn't fill that void my mother left. No matter how much I tried or what I did, he still wouldn't eat. It was clear that losing my mom was killing him.

Then he started staying out late, hanging with his so-called "friends." It was his attempt to stay away from home, probably because it all reminded him of what he had lost. I guess what he wasn't aware of was that he had a teenaged son who was dealing with loneliness himself. My brother was in college, so most of the time, I was home alone. (This probably contributes to my desire to be alone now. I genuinely love people, but most of the time, I actually prefer to be by myself). He was becoming distant and more isolated from us. I guess my uncle or my brother told him how I was feeling—because we started having more conversations about it. We became closer and started having manlier, heart-to-heart discussions. I realized he had been looking for someone to fill the void my mother left. Honestly, I think that in some way or another, we all were doing the same. But mom's void couldn't be filled. Dad felt guilty for not trying hard enough to convince my late mom not to go ahead with the surgery. His guilt consumed him, and even though we began to get closer, he still looked for a way to cope with the pain.

My father then started being irresponsible, spending money carelessly. This was another attempt to shield the pain and push the hurt away, but it did not help. It was destroying him instead. He began living a lavish lifestyle with the insurance money paid to him after mom's death. He would buy a lot of fancy suits and hang out with friends, paying for all their bills. Those friends were untrustworthy and fake. They deceived him, telling him all the things he wanted to hear. They told him that they would always be there for him. They would go on and on about how they would look after him and his family. My father has passed now, and I haven't seen any of those friends since his funeral, even so much as to find out how we were faring. As an adult, I reflect on my mother's passing and my father's undeserving trust in people. As he looked for healing, he neglected the truth and, ultimately, his overall health. I began to feel as though, mentally, I was losing the person I needed most. However, I could have never prepared for what came next.

A few months after Mom's death, my father was diagnosed with cancer. I watched painfully as the days passed, and the flesh fell from his bones. He lost a lot of weight—about 60 to 70 pounds. He started chemotherapy, and he tried to hide it from me. Chemotherapy did well for him at first. He became stronger and started doing better, but that was short-lived. The cancer came back even stronger than it was before. At that time, we started living with my uncle (my father's brother) and aunt due to my father's decline in health. During this time, my uncle brought me into the living room, and I remember having one of the most difficult conversations I ever had to have. Without saying too much, he said so much. My uncle was telling me that I needed to decide if I wanted to continue living with him or move with my other aunt in Huntsville. This ultimately meant my father wouldn't make it. I was 16 years old then, closing out my sophomore year of high school. Most teenagers were deciding which college they wanted to attend when they would get their first car or who they would ask to prom, but I was mentally preparing to bury my father just shortly after burying my mother. My father wanted my uncle to look after me, as they were really close, so I told my uncle I would continue to stay with him.

My dad died on the night of May 25, 2005. I will never forget that night with all the sadness it brought. Everybody was expecting it to happen, but it didn't change the fact that when it finally did, it was painful for us. It was especially painful for me because deep down, I hoped and prayed that he would get better. He was my Superman. He taught me that nothing should ever hold me down, and until my mom's death, no one thought that anything could hold him down. The depression got to him and held him down, paving the way for the cancer to do the same. I remember the nights I would go for football practice and then stay up late with him. He was always in excruciating pain; seeing him in that condition broke my heart. I remember the times I would go to his room and stay with him, just holding his hand. I remember the times he would wake up in the middle of the night because of a bad dream or because he was hungry. I was there the whole time, and I watched as he suffered. It was agonizing and a lot to deal with. My hero was dying, and I could do nothing but hope and pray.

When Dad eventually died, a part of me died as well. You see, that's the thing about hope. When you've hoped for a long time for something, and it doesn't come to pass, that hope shatters. That's what happened to me. I became like a turtle, and I hid in my shell. I completely shut down. I didn't want to let anyone in. I began to act out at school and everywhere else. I was not myself. I got into so much trouble at school because I was angry and lashed out all the time. The people at school, including the principal and the teachers, couldn't understand what was going on with me. I became the "angry black kid," being so aggressive in school. I can't help but wonder that if my skin color was lighter, would they have sought a therapist or additional help for me?

No matter how they tried, no one fully understood what I had been through or what I was currently going through. I didn't think they would understand. I didn't believe any of them could relate. I spiraled out of control and got suspended from school. This just added to my depression. No one tried to connect with me on a personal level to help. They were quick to label me negatively instead of offering help, and it was uncomfortable. No one sent me to counseling. No one, other than my uncle and my aunt, tried talking to me. No one tried to get me professional help. I was dealing with a lot, and I was doing it all alone. I was at constant war with myself, losing but trying to win.

I was very misunderstood and frequently labeled. I had to be strong, or at least pretend to be. I would smile a lot, but deep inside, I was hiding my scars. Even as I write this, the surface of my desk is full of tears. I have had to pause several times when writing this story because even now—16 years later—it's still painful at times. It hurts to know that, even as a kid, you can truly be alone in this cold world. I'm forever grateful to my uncle and aunt because they tried their best to be there for me, making things easier and trying so hard to make life a lot simpler. But I was just a boy then. I didn't know how to deal with everything that was happening. I remember how the kids would make fun of me, calling me a "homeless bastard" and even going further to write my name on the bleachers next to those same words. They said all kinds of terrible things to and about me. Sometimes, it's hard to think that children those ages could be so incredibly cruel, but that was exactly the case. The kids who were supposed to be my friends were the

20

same ones making fun of and insulting me, and they had no idea how that hurt me. Tell me, what could be crueler than that? The pain only continued as time passed. I struggled whenever the holidays were due. I didn't have a father or a mother, and both Father's and Mother's Days were a bitter reminder of this as well as the memory of this painful loss. It was the same with Christmas and Thanksgiving. Back then, I didn't see anything to be thankful for, but now, I find gratitude for many things, especially having my aunt and my uncle in my life.

My aunt and my uncle are like parents to me. If you didn't know us, you would probably think that my uncle is my dad. We favor each other a lot, and I have taken on a lot of his characteristics. This is not a bad thing, as he's one of the greatest men I have ever met. My hope is that one day I can be half as good of a man as he is. During my senior year of high school, I rebelled against him. I had so much built-up anger, which I didn't know how to deal with. I left home for a while and went to live with another aunt, my mom's sister. The next few months were even tougher for me. I felt locked in a cage. However, graduation came around, and I was excited to be leaving Winterboro High School. I was headed to college at Auburn University in Montgomery. Finally, I was going to be officially on my own. After all, mentally, I felt I was already living solo. No one would be looking over my shoulder. I was going to be able to do whatever I wanted, whenever I wanted. So that is just what I did.

During my freshman year in college, I partied and skipped all of my morning classes. This may come as a shocker to some, but I actually flunked out of college. Yes, I flunked out. I had "F's" all across my transcript. Needless to say, what was supposed to be the best time of my life created more anxiety and depression. I decided that maybe I should just give up on school because it just wasn't for me. I did not want to return home to my family and let everyone know I had failed, so I hid it. At the time, I was dating a girl from that way, and she had a private dorm room in the west courtyards. I stayed with her while working valet at the casino in Shorter. I don't think my classmates thought much of it because they were used to seeing me visiting anyway, but none of them had a clue that I was no longer in school. Valet actually gave me an opportunity to make pretty good money at the time because the casino was new and steadily adding things around, such as hotels and restaurants. However, I had hopes of possibly being a probation officer, and I did not want to be chasing cars for the rest of my life.

After a stern conversation with my brother, I decided I was going to transfer to Alabama A&M University. After all, this was the school I was planning to attend from the start. In the summer of 2009, I left my life in Montgomery and headed for Huntsville, Alabama. Alabama A&M is where things really started to shape up for me. I got a chance to play college football which was always my dream. I started focusing on myself and enjoying my HBCU experience. I met several good people and friends who eventually became family. I had my share of ups and downs like everyone else, but I made memories and friends that I am forever grateful for. In 2013, I graduated with a Bachelor of Science in Physical Education. In 2018, I graduated with a Masters of Arts in Secondary Teacher Education from the University of Phoenix-Online.

One of my greatest college memories is meeting the girl who would become my wife at Bibb Graves Hall in 2010. She was the smartest person in class, and I surely wasn't. I thought the best decision I could make was to befriend her. We began texting and conversing, and it seemed like one day, all of a sudden, we were falling in love. Alabamians are known for shutting the state down during snow days, and on one random day, that's exactly what happened. A snow day turned into a date at O'Charley's and eventually into a wonderful marriage. We are complete opposites, but they say opposites attract. My wife helped me by being a true friend. She never wanted anything from me. All she wanted was just for me to be the best me. She is beautiful outwardly, but her inner beauty shines even brighter. In her, I found something so genuine and rare. She saw something in me that I didn't see in myself. She encouraged me, even at a young age, and helped me to never give up. Having the love of your life and best friend in one is something I will forever be grateful for. Life gets hard, but with God and the right people in your corner, you can keep going. You can and will survive.

I'm also grateful to my wife's family. They have become like a second family to me, and I don't have to spend Christmas and Thanksgiving in bitterness and agony anymore, regretting the past. They helped me enjoy the holiday seasons and just having fun again. I'm so close with my wife's family, and it is always very lovely being around them. They are part of my outlet. They are intelligent, goofy, and very chill. Like any family, they have some problems, which usually make for good stories. We always have a good time, though. They really should have their own TV show. They have some of the best stories you would ever hear. Seeing how close my wife's family is makes me value my family relationships even more. My brother and I are closer than ever. We hang out and talk every chance we get. We don't talk every day, but we are always there for each other whenever needed. I love him dearly and know that I can always count on him. He truly inspires me with how much vision he has for his future and his outlook on life. I love the fact that he just lives his life. He doesn't worry about little things. He just packs his bag and goes. It makes me laugh just thinking about it. He's so much like mom, and I am more like dad. I cherish the bond we have and how that has helped me over the years.

If you're reading this story, I need you to know that you're not alone in your struggles. So many people love you. So many people are ready to help you. Take your time, as long as you need, to deal with whatever you are going through. However, do not let it destroy you. Do not let people tell you how long it takes to heal. I wouldn't even dare tell you that time heals all wounds completely. It has been nearly 20 years for me, and I still feel the hurt. Like I mentioned before, I cried a lot while writing this book, especially on my story. What I can say is; time will make it hurt a little less each day, month, or year. Time will help you deal with it, but the bulk of the work has to be done by you. You need to wake up each day with the intent of being better. Find someone to talk to. It doesn't have to be a family member. I know how hard it is to talk to a family member about a particular issue you're going through sometimes. Find someone you can open up to, and if you need to cry, do it. Cry as much as you need to feel better. I know I'm still struggling with my issues, but feel free to reach out to me. I'd be more than happy to help while you are getting through whatever it is you're going through. We could figure it out together. I'll tell you a secret that I'd have preferred to have kept a secret if not for this book. I was suicidal. At one point in my life, I decided it was better to be dead than to live in sadness and agony. I'm grateful to God for not allowing me to go forward with those thoughts. I'm writing this now because I don't want to live that way anymore, and I don't want you to think that way anymore either. I want to be happy and free, and I want the same for you. I recommend Jesus Christ in your life. Quite frankly, He's the only one capable of giving you that happy and free life. He is the one who gave it to me. He picked me up from the gutter and helped me put my life back on track. It was after I completely surrendered my life to him that I began to be joyful again.

There is so much joy in Jesus Christ, just waiting for you to tap into it. It's because of Christ's impact on my life that I have committed myself to helping others who are struggling with living, just as I did. I know sometimes you're not happy with your life. You may still struggle through all the hurt and pain, fighting to find a way to smile. I need you to know that if you feel sad and frustrated, it's okay. It's okay to be sad. It's okay to be hurt. It's okay to feel frustrated. Don't listen to the people who say you should not show your emotions or that you should hide them behind a smile. People cope with different situations in different ways, and we need to learn to accept that. There's nothing wrong with that as long as you don't jeopardize yourself in the process. God has you. He's that friend, family member, counselor, or therapist, waiting for you to reach out to Him and open up. It is not an easy thing to do, I know. It requires strength and commitment each day. Though it won't be easy, I know that we can get through this with the help of each other. I know that, despite the obstacles in our path, we will rise as conquerors. I never wanted to go through what I went through. I never asked for any of it. I never asked to still struggle with things. However, because I did, I can help someone else overcome their despair. I am not the first person to go through this, and I won't be the last. Maybe if I had heard someone else's story that overcame what I went through, it would have helped me. I am hoping that my testimony will help someone and maybe even save a life. I am on this journey daily, and while I am better than I was, I am still not where I will be. If I had no hurt in my life, I wouldn't be able to experience healing. Since I know hurt personally, I also have the blessing of knowing healing. There is peace after the storm. No matter what you are going through, I leave you with this phrase:

No Hurt, No Healing
Know Hurt, Know Healing
I pray you continue to fight despair in your pursuit to fulfill your destiny.

Remember, you are not alone in this.

Hiding My Truths

It's hard to tell my story after struggling to get over it. Knowing it will be published makes it even more difficult. I was raped by a family member when I was only 13 years old. Like most teenagers my age, I was still a confused girl entering puberty and learning more about myself. This just made the whole experience even more horrifying. The assault made me shut down. I felt so numb. It was as though I had started living in a shell. I was hurt, ashamed, angry, guilty, sad, and confused. However, I managed to lock all those feelings away. I became an outsider to myself, smiling and laughing but not feeling anything. My outer emotions did not reveal the truth. It was as if I wore a mask to shield everything I felt. Each time I looked in the mirror, a stranger stared back at me. Church didn't help. I went to service every Sunday and listened to the preacher talk about how God would take care of me, but it just didn't help. I continued to feel a particular hatred and disappointment for men. No one knew what was going on with me. I didn't talk about the rape or how it affected me because I knew that doing so would make it all real. At the time, I preferred to live in denial. I wanted to pretend none of it happened. I was doing a good job at hiding my truths. If no one knew about it, my life would be easier. I thought it was the right thing to do and the best way to get over it. So, I continued to live that way.

I completed high school and got into college. I met several nice guys, but by default, I didn't get close to any of them. I was so fearful. I even refused to intern with them. I tried therapy, but just like church, it didn't help either. After a few sessions of therapy, I decided that the best solution for me was to leave the city. I believed if I moved away, my problems would somehow stay behind, and I would finally be free. Did this work? No. I couldn't outrun my issues because they were a part of me. I couldn't escape myself. I started having horrible nightmares and vivid replays of my trauma. This was when I hit rock bottom. I couldn't handle it, and I felt like I would explode. Finally, one night I called a trusted friend and narrated everything to her. It felt good to finally release all of the things I held inside.

My friend was a good listener, and most of all, she was so nice and understanding about the whole thing. She encouraged me to tell my parents, but I was scared. I didn't know how they would react or how they would look at me. Would they treat me the same? The feelings I had locked away all those years ago came flooding back. I became engulfed with so much shame and guilt. I thought it was my fault and that my parents would

29

see it that way too. You see, it was my uncle, my mother's brother, who assaulted me. This caused me to live in fear, thinking my parents would not believe me. I assumed they would call me a liar, and I did not want that. Besides, my coming clean would only stir up family drama, and I just couldn't handle the trouble. With that in mind, I decided to remain silent. At that point, my trusted friend became my only solace. We talked a lot, and she was always ready to listen. I realized that there was so much I had bottled up inside. Once I opened up to her, it all started spilling out. The emotions were overwhelming. As a result, I was despondent and spent a lot of time in bed. There was no motivation in me to do anything. I didn't even want to do basic things such as taking a shower, getting dressed, or cleaning my room. I completely let myself go.

I decided to make myself less attractive so that men would never want me again. I hated my body. What others saw as a blessing became a curse. Most women would spend their fortune for the kind of body I possessed. Nevertheless, because of the pain and trauma I endured, I despised it. I didn't want to live like this, so I thought about suicide oftentimes. Thinking about the years ahead of me made me panic. I was depressed, sad, and lonely. I couldn't fathom spending the rest of my life being miserable. I had to kill myself. I didn't care if I went to hell; surely, hell would be better than what I was going through. I decided I would tell my parents about the rape so they would understand my "why" after I was dead. I needed them to understand why I couldn't go on. I stayed up the whole night penning my will, along with a suicide note and goodbye letters. I picked up the bottle of pills I had hidden in my dresser. I intended to take them, but for some reason, I called my friend instead. I poured out my heart, crying as I told her what I was about to do. It was past midnight, but she drove over to my place right away. She sat with me, talking while I listened. She convinced me to put the pills away and go to sleep. She told me she wouldn't tell anyone about what I almost did, but she lied. She told my parents the next day. At the time, I saw her action as a betrayal, a sign that she didn't care about me. I know better now. She did what was best for me. I understand today how hard it must have been for her to go behind my back and tell my parents. At the time, however, I was furious. I hated her for it and cursed myself for telling her any of it in the first place. Instead of talking, I felt that I should have just finished the job.

My parents drove me to the hospital as soon as they found out, and I was admitted to the psychiatric unit for intensive care. I was diagnosed with post-traumatic stress disorder (PTSD) and major depressive disorder (MDD). It was one of the worst nights of my life. I felt violated. It was as though I had done something wrong, and I was being punished for it. They took away everything I had come in with, including my clothes. I had to wear hospital scrubs instead. I felt so uncomfortable being there. Every day, the unit was filled with doctors, nurses, and psychologists. Every now and then, someone would outright ask me why I was there. Then came the "How are you feeling" inquiries. I hated the blunt questions or having to say anything at all. I eventually came to realize that the more I remained silent about my feelings, the longer I would stay in the unit. I didn't want to stay any longer than I had to. Being there already was overwhelming for me to bear. I grew up in a religious home where I was accustomed to only wearing skirts.

At the facility, I had to wear pants, coupled with the fact that the guys and girls were mixed. I attended an all-girls school up until college, so constantly being there with men was difficult. I cried nonstop on my first day but eventually adjusted. I also became accustomed to the very annoying rules, like having a nurse go with me to the bathroom. Though, to my surprise, there were some parts of my hospital stay I enjoyed, such as group therapy. It felt good getting to talk to other people who were going through similar situations. They understood me. I began to feel safe in the environment. At home, I had a constant fear that someone was after me.

Once I began appreciating the experience and its benefits, I was able to open up without fear.

After a week, I was discharged. I felt more comfortable talking about what happened to me when I was 13 years old. I learned to communicate my feelings at the hospital, which was very beneficial in my healing process. I started seeing a follow-up psychologist who specialized in trauma. I also went to group therapy once a week, although things didn't get better as quickly as I'd hoped. I was still depressed and suicidal. This led me to overdose twice on pills. My parents wanted to send me back to the intensive care unit but ended up taking me to a psychiatrist who prescribed anti-depressants. I didn't want to take the pills, but the doctor explained that the medication would stabilize me and help in my down moments. The next week, I put all my razors, pills, and negative things in a box and got rid of them. It felt so good. I felt so strong. I switched to a therapist I preferred and got closer to my therapy group. I was able to open up and talk to them, and they became like a second family to me.

Now, I look forward to group therapy. It's such a great place to talk about things and get support. I still have a lot to work through. My parents constantly are frustrated with me because I have trouble communicating and being open with them. However, we all try to make it a point to understand each other. My friends have been incredible too. They have each loved and supported me through my healing process. My therapist is still currently assisting me in putting the pieces of my life together—patching up my relationship with my parents, helping me feel good about myself, and encouraging me to complete school. Looking ahead still scares me, but this time, I lift my head and stare down the road, knowing I must move forward. There is a light at the end of the tunnel. I am confident knowing if I can get through this, I can do anything. There will be no stopping me. I also know God is with me every step of the way. I have faith in Him like never before, and I know he won't let me down. He has helped me through all of this because He has faith in me too. He believes I'm strong and capable. I won't let him down… I won't let myself down. I will not let my past control who I become in the future. Every day I let past circumstances ruin my life, the more significant it became. I want to share my story so that others going through similar situations know that they are not alone.

Many people wonder how I got to this point, where I can sincerely say I am in a better place. The truth is, life didn't get easier; nonetheless, I got stronger. I was only able to truly begin the healing process by realizing what I was lacking all those years—acceptance. Even though I went to church, sought counseling, and talked to friends and family, I still dealt with suicidal thoughts and depression. This was because , I never truly faced what happened to me at such a young age. Once I fully accepted what happened and stopped living in denial, I was able to begin the process of healing completely. After wholly taking in what transpired, I then had to accept that it wasn't my fault. Often times when bad things happen, we put some blame on ourselves, even when unsubstantiated. Unknowingly, I did the same thing for years. That is why I "let myself go" physically and hid the terror from my parents for so long. I believed that a family member only chose to assault me because I must have played a role in his decision. Prior to this encounter, my uncle seemed like the average guy, always appearing kind and caring. I would mentally obsess over what I did to make him do what he did. I realized over time that his decision was just that…HIS DECISION! I now understand that it wasn't my fault. Accepting this pushed me to become better mentally.

My next stage of acceptance was realizing that I needed help. Once I came face to face with the extent of my pain and the fact that I really wanted to get better, I was able to tap into a new level of healing. It's one thing to "say" you want to heal and another to actually participate fully in that process. After taking the time to truly engage in my recovery and all that came with it—getting closer to God, working with my therapist, and beginning to forgive—restoration began to reveal itself in my life. Finally, I had to accept that God still had a plan for me. My job on this Earth is not done yet. I now know that my story can and will be used to help others who may have gone through similar situations. If you are reading this, don't let your situation control who you become. You can decide to take every situation and make it the best. You can and will overcome. Never give up! Accept that you will be who you are destined to be.

*"God grant me the serenity to **accept** the things I cannot change, the courage to change the things I can, and the wisdom to know the difference."*

Don't Fake the Funk

Life has a way of taking you to a mountaintop, then forcing you to make a lifetime decision to jump or fly. I chose to fly. Life was great. I had been in church my entire life, and I knew all about Christ. At least, that's what I thought. I watched my mother pray every chance she got while my father brought forth the word in church. However, it wasn't until I needed the Lord for myself that I found out my doubts outweighed my faith. It is one thing to listen to the word and another to exercise it in your personal life.

This was my second marriage. The first had been destroyed by lies, deception, and infidelity. I thought I was healed and delivered from it. I was joyful and excited. This was the happiest I had been in a long time. Everything seemed to be going well this time around. I believed this would be the perfect marriage. We seemed to be more equally yoked. We both grew up in church, my dad being a minister and his father-figure being a pastor. We knew the word of God and what was right and wrong in His eyes. We seemed to have it all figured out. In my head, this marriage was going to be easy. If we prayed every night and lived our lives right, everything would be alright. Why wouldn't it be?

I found out rather too early that being in church doesn't make you a Christian. Attending church doesn't even scratch the surface of having a personal relationship with God. My wedding came and went. Then, reality set in. My husband and I were living our best, blessed life when the problems started. We began fighting and having frequent disagreements. We even stopped praying together. I had all these ideas in my head about how my new marriage would work. This wasn't how I imagined things to turn out at all. In the midst of our daily arguments, I discovered that he was cheating. Finding this out hit me like a ton of bricks. I couldn't grasp what went wrong in the relationship or how it got to that point. I was furious, upset, and above all, heartbroken. I became a woman who trusted no one. I prayed to God to heal my brokenness. Little did I know He was only strengthening me for the trials ahead of me.

I had gone from being this vibrant, happy, carefree single woman to being a now miserable, broken and depressed married woman. I was lost and felt empty. For many months, I came to church with an enormous void, hiding behind the true hurt and pain I was feeling. During the service, I'd lift my hands even though I didn't feel a thing. I still said amen when, in all honesty, I just wanted to run to the bathroom and cry until the service was over. It was my sad attempt to pretend that everything was ok. I was painting a perfect image to the public while inside, I was broken and ashamed. I lost my authenticity trying to "fake the funk." I was, as my friend Marty would say, "smiling but scarred." I knew that I couldn't go on this way. Surely, my purpose was a lot greater than my pain. So, with the intent to live better than I had been doing so far, I went on my knees in prayer once more. My strength began to grow. I needed faith more than ever. Faith, as my parents would often quote from the Bible, didn't need to be any bigger than a mustard seed to work great miracles in one's life. I mustered up enough strength to find that faith, even if only just as big as a mustard seed. Then, God began to restore me. My inner self had become so weak that I began to conform to the ways of the world. But shame the devil; my pain was purposeful. God was developing my purpose through all of the hardships and trials I was enduring. As I began to overcome and realize who I truly was called to be, I was reminded of a song by Kirk Franklin that said, "My pain was preparation for my destiny." I knew it was time for me to see that even though I didn't know what it was, God had a plan for me.

In 2017, I decided to rise and be unapologetically me—the authentic me God created. That was when He began to deliver me from my pain and hurt. I asked God to forgive me for not being true to myself and for not being true to Him. At that moment, I completely related to the verse of "Amazing Grace" that says, "I once was lost but now am found." Do not let things that ultimately did not go as planned allow you to isolate yourself from God. Sometimes our plans are not His plans, and we must remember He is all-knowing and omnipotent. Therefore, always cling to your faith and stay true to God and yourself. Often, bad situations are meant to strengthen us and give us a testimony so that we can help others going through similar circumstances. These blessings in disguise give us a cause to glorify God at the end of it all.

During my divorce, I came to realize that pretense only made my life more puzzling. While I pretended to be ok and pretended to be someone I truly was not, I only became more broken. I was unable to put the pieces of my life back together until I fully sought God's purpose and plan. You see, you can't be purposeful while pretending because He needs the real you! God knew who you were before you were formed, and He wants us to tap into that authenticity. There's no need for us to "fake the funk" because Christ knows our hearts, and he cares for us. I am always reminded of 1 Peter 5:7, which says, "Cast all your anxiety on Him, because He cares for you." This is exactly what we should do—cast our worries unto God.

Growing up in the Baptist church, I was taught as a young child to bring all your burdens to the Lord. While I truly believe that you should always do this and that God will be there for you, there is nothing wrong with seeking additional help. That is why I began spiritual counseling with leaders in my church to invest in becoming a better me. I discovered that most times in my life, God used other people to give me the revelation that I needed. After participating in spiritual counseling for a while, I developed a different love for myself. I discovered a new purpose and was ready to plant myself on a solid ground. I made a career change and did something I always wanted to do. Before, I felt like fear and wanting to please everyone else held me back.

I decided that I would no longer live for anyone else. In my new career, I discovered a new area of ministry that I was passionate about. I am now using my testimony to help bring light to those who feel that others have thrown them away. For so long, I felt unloved, neglected, and unsure of myself. Especially after two divorces, I felt unworthy. However, how could I be unworthy if my Father in heaven created me? I am confident that God will use my hardships and difficult times to help someone else, just the way my spiritual leaders helped me. I no longer have to "fake the funk." I am genuinely living my best life, and I am doing it for myself.

The Lonely Road of Life

In 2006, a couple of friends and I started a group. We wrote songs together, sang together, ate together, and even laughed and cried together. We were very close. It was more than just a singing group. We were brothers. Personally, I finally felt like I belonged. With them, I didn't feel out of place, and I knew that God strategically put me there. I have learned, though, that God often places us in situations to prepare us for our next step in life. However, about ten years later, I found myself at a standstill. I felt stuck. The quest to fulfill my destiny started weighing heavily on me. I had to take a step back and ask myself if I was on the right path. While at this standstill, frustration began creeping in, so much so that it opened the door to doubt. This was uncharted territory for me as I began to see that getting to my destiny required that I leave the group. I prayed to God about it and vented to my wife, family, and friends. God was clearly communicating that I needed to leave, but it was such a big move for me to make. I doubted if I had what it took to make such move. We were all like brothers, after all. I thought waiting it out would make it better. Maybe it was just a storm that would pass, perhaps a test from God. So, I decided to stay put.

As time went on, things seemed to get tougher. God's voice became louder. God gave me directions, and I had to follow them. However, I hesitated. I knew this showed my lack of trust. Finally, I decided to heed God's voice and realized that it was time for a change. I chose to step out of the group. I didn't know where my new path was taking me, but I was not worried. You'd think that I'd go on to write about how I walked into my destiny and everything was great, but that's not exactly how it went. Life doesn't always work that way, at least not for me.

My huge step of faith led me straight into isolation. I found myself in a dark place, surrounded but lonely. I was on the lonely road of life. I was a married man with a huge family and several friends, but I was in a cocoon of alienation. I felt ungraceful, going from being a beautiful butterfly back to being a desolate caterpillar. It was strange, and I felt conflicted. I tried my best to be a light in this dark world. I continued to pretend that everything was normal. I would still smile and put on, laughing at jokes and hugging everyone as I typically would. But that was all fake. My world was dark. I continued to attend church every Sunday, serving God in my best capacity, but it didn't change the sense of loneliness that engulfed and crippled me. How could I explain to my wife that despite the love she had for me, and although I spoke with my best friend every day, I was in a place where I felt like I had no one I could truly depend on? No one understood how I felt; therefore, I was left carrying pain and agony that filled my days. My Saturdays that were once filled with songs and praises to God were now quiet with myself in my own thoughts. The devil tricked me on every level, wanting me to think I was lonesome and that people didn't care about me. He wanted me to believe that everything was hopeless and that I should give up on my dreams. I no longer spent my time listening to music, which was the one thing that made me happy. I pushed everything and everyone away. I lived in a bubble and was suffocating. With each passing moment, I felt myself drowning in my seclusion. The guys I had once called brothers were now strangers. We went from being a close family to barely communicating with each other. I was just a step away from my breaking point when I found God again.

I didn't find God on the back of a cereal box, and I didn't find him literally because God wasn't the one lost. When I found myself in a dark place, with the music and all of the noise tuned out, I realized he wanted to draw me nearer to Him. I remember it like it were yesterday. I was riding down the road quietly with no music. I asked God, "Lord, where are you?" How was I living this life alone, surrounded by so many people, yet feeling secluded and depressed? Suddenly, I remember being awakened by the call of my name. I had blacked out. Apparently, I had a pretty nasty car accident. I don't remember having the wreck, only waking up to being in pain with a sore neck and a broken arm. It was at the hospital that I "found" God again. Early one morning, while I was lying there by myself, I heard what I would describe as God's voice talking to me. I immediately started crying out because, like a turtle, I had been hiding in a shell. A powerful voice reminded me of a phrase that I will continue to take with me for the rest of my life. "You're never alone." For about the next ten minutes in that hospital bed, I cried and cried. I spent my whole life thinking that I needed others. When I didn't have anyone, I thought I was alone. I had forgotten that my Savior said He would never leave or forsake me. Not only did God remind me I was not alone, but He also gave me a "you are enough" attitude. I felt like I needed a group in order to be successful. I felt like walking away from the group would mean that I would never make it in the music industry. However, that night in the hospital bed, God did something for me. He sprung a writer's well in my belly.

Anointed to play keys since I was a teen, I never thought that I could be a writer. I thought it necessary to rely on others. However, after being isolated and having no one but God, something stirred up in me. Now, I use my ability to play, sing, and write music to inspire others who may feel like me. I'm working on establishing my own record company. I'm doing it with the help of God, my wife, and my son. I no longer feel lonely; I feel strength, and I feel loved. I began to truly seek God on a deeper level, believing that I could do all things through Christ. I started to grow closer to Him and rebuild my character. I blocked out all the noise in my head and focused on myself and the tasks in front of me. What I thought was remoteness trying to put me in depressed seclusion, was instead a time of reflection needed to realize that my identity is not found in others. I realized that my path wasn't about me at all. Destiny is not just a journey that reaches an ultimate end where you get to rest. It is a continuous voyage. I was walking into my destiny the whole time. I still do today. The people I have helped, as well as the people who helped me, my challenges, my failures, and my victories, are all a part of my story. I use my story to glorify God. Others and I have stepped out in faith. We're waiting on you to join us.

The Man I Was Meant to Be, Not the Man You See

I never really liked talking about being a fat kid. Being overweight put a dent in my feelings to a great extent while growing up. Sometimes, even now, as a grown man, I find myself struggling with self-esteem. My weight was never brought up as a topic of discussion in the family, probably because everyone in the family was overweight as well. We were one big happy family (literally and figuratively.) I know a lot of other families in which the parents make their children incredibly aware that they are overweight. These parents constantly talk to their kids about it and even go as far as hiding snacks from them. However, each family is different. As a kid, I was ignorant of the fact that there was "something wrong with me."

For as long as I can remember, I have been overweight. In all my pictures, from as early as two years old, I was larger in size. It was just the way I had always been. In my early years, I was unaffected by that fact because it hadn't occurred to me that there was something wrong with my weight. I was seven or eight years old when I first realized that my size made me different. It was my grandma who first made me see this. One day she took me upstairs to the family room and had me do exercises using home workout videos. She was a persuasive one, encouraging me to lose weight by offering money as an incentive. There was some predetermined number of sit-ups I had to do to receive the reward. My grandma singled me out because I was overweight for my age. I never talked about it, but it made me feel bad. It was the very first time I was ashamed of myself and the very first time I felt like I needed to change.

My bad experiences as a fat kid only continued to grow from there as I grew in size. After school or during field trips, I'd race to the bus so I could be the first one to get a seat. This was to avoid bumping into anyone as I shimmied my way through the aisles, hurrying to a seat. There was also this girl, Carly, whom I had a crush on. She was the most beautiful girl I had ever seen, at least for a third-grader. She always wore her hair in nice little braids, and her bows always matched her outfit. I knew she was special. She was brilliant as well, answering all the questions asked in class. I tried my best to befriend her, and she was nice to me. One day, I found a huge amount of courage and decided to write her a letter. There was no Instagram or Snapchat then, thus, this was how we communicated. In the letter, I expressed how much it meant for her to be my friend and how amazing I thought she was. She replied to my letter with one of her own, saying, "You are too fat." I'm not sure what hurt worse—being turned down or the insult that came with it. This just made me more and more aware of my size. I'd look forward to the days that I got to ride home with my granddad after school because it meant that I would skip the embarrassment of getting on the bus and the agony that came with trying to shrink myself to avoid touching the person who sat next to me. Even normal experiences, such as getting to my school desk, were a painful reminder of how fat I was. I was always conscious about who was around to see me struggle to get into the desk, and it was even more of a struggle getting out. I would wait until most of the class had cleared out before un-stuffing myself from the one-piece desks. During lunch, I'd give my lunch trays away because I didn't want people to make fun of me while I was eating. This continued all through my school years.

In the seventh, eighth, and ninth grades, I had several people I thought of as friends. Most of them were skinny. When they swapped shoes and clothes, I just stood there watching them, feeling left out and out of place. I was never able to wear a pair of cool shoes or clothes, seeing as my parents were not well off. I wore many things ranging from thrift store items to hand-me-downs mostly for adult men. I would cut my clothes tags before school so that my friends would not see what sizes I wore. My friends didn't directly tell me I didn't belong, but I felt it. They hung out without me a lot. They would also pass notes around in class all the time, but the notes never got to me. I didn't get invited to do things with them, and I knew it was because of my weight. I was different from them. I hated the few times I even got to hang out with them outside of school because I always got the feeling they were embarrassed to be seen with me. They would talk to me less when we were around other people or walk together and leave me behind as if they weren't with me. It was so hurtful back then, so much so that I remember the exact details of where and how these events took place. They were not good friends, but I didn't know that at the time. I was ignorant as to what a true friend was. If you have anyone in your life like these people I called friends, trust me, you're better off without them.

During that time, one of the guys on my baseball team had a birthday party. Everyone was making their way over to the table where the cake and ice cream were set up. I joined them in doing this. It was customary to sing the birthday song and then grab a piece of cake afterward. After the song, I reached in to grab a piece of cake when the mom of the celebrant reached across from where she stood and blocked my hands. She mumbled the words, "Maybe you should lay off the cake." It was a very cruel thing to say, especially coming from an adult like herself. I didn't tell my mother about this, but I knew if I did, she would start a war. The other kids must have heard her comment too because they all pointed at me and laughed.

This added to the hurt. Kids are bullies, but adults are no different sometimes. The feeling of being judged by others and treated differently because of your appearance doesn't just go away as you get older. It especially doesn't when it begins at an age when you aren't emotionally equipped to deal with it. One thing I found was that as the "fat kid," there is an ability to overlook the crappy way you are treated by others. You are in constant need of validation, wanting people to like you. You avoid drawing attention to yourself or causing any problems because being overweight is already a problem. That is already reason enough for people not to like you, so why add more? Or at least that's what I believed. When you are ten years old, having fake friends usually feels better than not having any. You learn to settle, just like I did, and the insecurities creep in.

You begin to think that your predicament is what you deserve, and you can't do anything to change it. This follows you all through your life, from childhood to adulthood, causing you to stay in toxic relationships. When you stay in toxic relationships, the less you think about yourself, and the more you continue to make bad decisions. It's a never-ending cycle. Every Christmas, I would pray not to get clothes as gifts—anything but clothes. Christmas gifts were a source of anxiety for me while growing up. I would receive clothes that didn't fit me but wouldn't say a word about it because I was too embarrassed. I felt ashamed that my family had to spend time considering how big I was as they picked out the clothing. I was bigger than they thought. I loved the stuff they picked out for me, but it only made me sad because I couldn't wear it. I felt trapped in myself. As a young guy in the school setting I was in, what you wore mattered. When I was 11, there was a time I was on the phone with my cousin. I heard the doorbell ring over the phone, and my cousin went to answer it. My cousin told whoever was at the door that she was on the phone with her cousin, and the girl asked, "The chunky one?" I felt bad, betrayed, and vulnerable as I realized that even my own family shared the rest of the world's opinion of me. This was my favorite cousin. She was supposed to defend me if someone attempted to make a mockery of my look. If she wouldn't defend me, who would?

As time went on, I tried my best to skip school. I would fake sickness or even make up lies to avoid going to school. I vividly recall fitness exams in physical education class. It's not something I will ever forget. I felt that it was the devil himself who came up with the exams. It was overwhelming for me—all the shuttle runs, push-ups, pull-ups, sit-ups, and mile runs. Struggling to do all of this was one of the most embarrassing occurrences of my life as a kid. There was no way I could successfully do pull-ups. The teachers had already failed me before I even began. My skinny friends excelled at these exams. Being skinny comes with the advantage of doing these exercises with ease. I did my very best to skip school on those days. I had plenty of experiences with kids coming up with plenty of jokes and insults for me, most of which lacked originality but still managed to affect me. Sadly, it wasn't only my peers who made me feel out of place. On my first day of gym class in high school, the PE teacher gave us a tour of the locker room and assigned us our lockers. In front of the whole class, he looked at me and pointed to the shower room and said, "There are bathroom stalls in there with doors, so you'll be more comfortable changing into your gym clothes." I felt bad, but I don't believe, even to this day, that his intentions were bad. The coach and I were pretty cool, but what he said that day is something I'll never forget because I immediately became an object of jokes and laughter. I felt like my body was a bad thing that should always be hidden, and for years onward, I never changed in front of another person again.

Many don't know this about me, but baseball was my first love. I enjoyed being part of a team. I wasn't the best at it, but I did it because I enjoyed it. Nevertheless, I'd purposely hesitate to leave the house for practice. I did this so I could be a few minutes late to avoid the first few minutes of running drills. It wasn't because I didn't want to run. It was because I didn't want my friends and parents who were still lingering around to see me running, especially if those parents were ones I had previously overhead making indirect comments about my weight to other parents or their children by suggesting I play certain positions or, like one parent did, not even play at all. At those times, I wished more than anything that they could have waited until I was out of earshot to say those things. I started getting tougher and adopting defense mechanisms to help me cope—not only with how others treated me but with how I felt about myself too. I learned quickly not to be too sensitive to comments made about me.

 By the time high school was in full swing, I had taken on the I-am-so-tough-and-don't-care-if-anyone-likes-me attitude. I developed a finely tuned sense of humor and became well-versed in sarcasm. I told more jokes about myself. I got into football and slimmed down. That is what a big boy was supposed to do. I began to love football because, surprisingly, I was good at it. Now the same people who made fun of me in elementary school were the ones who needed me to protect them on the football field. I instantly became very popular because—when you are the guy who protects the most popular kids in school, they seem to love you. We fat kids learn to compensate by being funny, smart, or, sometimes, mean—anything that makes you relevant. I took on a version of all of these at some point in time in high school. Putting yourself down or putting someone else down first seemed like a pretty good way to prevent others from having the chance to do it to you. It worked most of the time. I made a core group of friends who are still my friends to date. I don't have a lot of friends, though. I realized that the smaller my inner circle, the easier life was. I did fun things and had plenty of normal experiences like the other kids. I was, for the most part, well-liked and never without something to do or people to hang out with during the weekends. I also had one of the nicest cars in the parking lot. I was big, so my parents got me an SUV.

I was popular enough, went to parties, proms, and school dances, and did things I wasn't supposed to do. It was all a normal teenage experience. My friends were good ones. They didn't make me feel out of place with them. It was my insecurities that did that. I just knew I'd rather avoid situations in which my weight would be a source of embarrassment. It was a mentality I carried for the rest of my life, a difficult one to shake even now that I have lost a lot of weight. I sat on the sidelines while growing up because of that insecure little boy who made a home inside of me and rattled around in my head, telling me I didn't belong because of my size. I felt anxious, uncomfortable, and not myself around people. My weight was out of control at that time. If I thought that way about myself, then surely, others thought the same. This only made it difficult for me to talk to anyone, even those that I loved.

I love and have always loved being around my extended family. They are some of my favorite people, and I know someday I will wish I had back the years I skipped going on holidays with them and the time I wasn't fully present when I did go. I just didn't feel good enough about myself to think that others would enjoy being around me. Over time, I realized that I was so focused on the negative things to the degree that I missed out on the good. Aside from my weight and the damaging words that came with it, I had a pretty typical childhood. I was loved, taken care of, and supported. My parents ensured I never lacked anything. They made me see a lot of qualities about myself that I take pride in today. As I matured, I decided to turn the negative into positive by identifying areas of growth that resulted from my weight journey. I am a lot less angry and resentful now compared to when I first realized what a significant amount of work I had to do if I wanted to be healthy. While being the fat kid isn't something I would wish on any other child, and while I don't particularly enjoy the fact that I dealt with some of the things I had to, I am also not sure I would change any of it now if I could. Being the "fat kid" gave me life lessons I wouldn't have had otherwise. I am who I am today because of it and because I overcame it. It taught me to be observant and perceptive, not only of other people's feelings but mine as well. I know what it's like to be treated unfairly, and now I am accepting and kind to all people, regardless of who they are or what they look like.

I taught myself to understand nutrition and health and why they are important. These were things I probably wouldn't have had to do if I weren't obese. I am conscious of how my words impact people, especially after being the target of cruel words said by others. I am glad to say that I am truly happy now. I even married a stunning woman. She could easily have been a model if she wanted to. We fell in love in college and have been married for five years now. I'm not sure if she noticed, but for a while, I was ashamed of undressing in front of her. I didn't want to feel humiliated again, and even though she didn't make me feel bad about myself, the fat kid effect still lived in my mind. I share this story because I don't want anyone to allow the hurt from their past to rule their present and future. My wife has only lifted me, and she compliments me daily. It does make me feel good to know that someone is very attracted to me. In the past, I couldn't imagine I'd ever find love like this. I couldn't, in my wildest imagination, picture someone loving me this way other than my family. We are expecting our second child any day now. Probably, by the time you are reading this, that child will be running around with our first child. Because I learned the importance of health by dealing with being overweight, I look forward to teaching my kids the importance of a balanced diet and exercise. Hopefully, this will be passed on to their kids, and their kids, and so on. I went through it, so my kids won't have to.

I recounted this story because I believe there is a kid or an adult out there struggling the same way I did. It could be you currently reading this or someone you know. Whatever the case may be, I just want to let you know that you are beautiful and you're special. You matter more than you can possibly think, and it doesn't matter what others think. The opinion of others doesn't define who you are. Remember, you are unique. Remember the words of the psalmist in Psalm 139:14, "I praise you, Lord, because I am fearfully and wonderfully, made; your works are wonderful, I know that full well." David understood that God had designed him in a special light, as He has done for you. You don't have to hide in the shadows, trying not to be noticed. You are a gift from God. The Bible says that every perfect gift comes from Him. Love yourself. You are perfect in your imperfections.

Who Can Mend My Broken Heart

They say you think you know people…well, until you marry them. It's a cliché, yes, and everybody says it, but you never fully understand it until you get married yourself. I met her in the summer of 1995—amidst good music, dancing, and alcohol—and it was beautiful. She was beautiful. She knew so much for someone so little, and that was intriguing to me. We spoke every night over the phone, and we couldn't get enough of each other. My phone bill rose with all of the long hours spent talking. As I took a serious look at the bill before I paid, I told myself, "For Tamia." Tamia. That was her name—the petite woman with the blonde hair and facial features to die for who had stolen my heart. We attended the same college, Ohio State University. I was two years older than her and couldn't for the life of me remember ever seeing her on campus. She said it was okay since we both took our studies quite seriously. I graduated with a Cumulative Grade Point Average of 4.0, while she graduated with a 3.9. I remember thinking, *Finally, someone worth my salt.* Salt was brainpower.

We spoke about everything—heaven, hell, politics, farming, recessions, life, love—and she was never out, never needing to catch up with me. She'd come over; we'd get to talking, and before I knew it, we were devouring each other on the couch. Whatever VHS movie was playing

59

would just be receding in the background. I know I wanted this forever. I planned our lives over in my head. Finally, I decided to make this woman my wife. With one knee on the ground and a ring in my right hand, I told her I wanted to marry her. She shrieked and held out her hand in excitement as I put the ring on it lovingly. Then I picked her up and told her she'd better say yes, so she couldn't wiggle out of it later. She laughed loudly. I loved this woman. I fell more in love with her with each passing day. I was convinced she was my soulmate. So, we got married. We had a huge wedding right out of my family's pocket. I purchased for her an even more giant wedding ring. It was much larger than the one I'd gotten for the engagement, although her friends had already "awed and oohed" over it.

She whispered to her mother that it felt a little heavy on her hand sometimes, to which her mother replied, "Stop showing off, Tamia. One more, and I'm swapping it with the one your father gave me." I thought it was funny as her father bellowed, "Hey!" and all of us fell into a fit of laughter. We said our vows and yeses in excitement and couldn't wait for the pastor's "you may now kiss the bride" before devouring ourselves. Our pastor's voice was just like that VHS—as it began to recede in the background. It felt like only us at that moment.

We spent our honeymoon traveling, and we explored all the places she ever wanted to go—Italy, the Bahamas, India, and Mexico. She had the taste. I had the money, and so we went. We ate Italian ice cream, danced with the crowds on Latina beaches, and knelt to pray in Israel. Then we returned home. Our honeymoon was amazing. The first few years of our marriage were excellent despite minor changes bound to come with living with someone. Our jobs were so demanding. We would both come back home exhausted, with dinner most nights being takeout. We realized a lot of money was going down the drain. As a result, we started what we called "cooking weekend," where we cooked food for the whole week on Saturday.

This gave us the opportunity to spend more quality time with each other while saving money. Our ultimate goal was to continue exploring the world. We planned to purchase a vacation home on the beach with a pontoon boat before we were too old to enjoy it. We eventually stopped cooking weekends. I guess work got in the way. We always seemed too tired, so some type of excuse always came up. At this point, we were still having intimacy and it remained great—mind-blowing even. I used to tease her about how we'd still be this crazy, deep into old age, and she'd break into hysterical laughter. We were funny like that. We both seemed to always enjoy each other. You could bet when we were together, we were always going to laugh and have a good time. Everyone always enjoyed being around us because our marriage seemed so perfect and fun. It was full of laughter. After three years of marriage, God blessed us to be parents to two wonderful kids.

We had a daughter and a son and named them Jennifer and Gary, respectively. Gary was over-energetic from the start, kicking and screaming as he came out and making the most noise in the hospital through the night. Jennifer was extremely serene. Sometimes I wondered if she was alive, but there she was, sleeping the whole time. They grew up like that—Gary, the talkative sportsman, and Jennifer, always quiet, observant, listening and watching intently with her legs crossed. I loved my baby girl. I still do.

Seven years into parenthood, I was the more active parent. Tamia would come home late, tired, and always blamed it on her work volume at the office. I was quiet any time she said so. Late became later, and tired became more tired. At first, I would stay up all night and wait for her to come home. After a while, I started saying a special prayer for her and going to sleep right after I put our kids to bed. One night, she came back from work drunk. I was up late, watching TV. I simply stared as she staggered in, and our eyes met. She let out a long, loud laugh and dropped her things on the table in the living room. I shrugged and continued watching TV as she continued her shaky steps inside. When I went to bed, she was already asleep with her back turned. I walked back to the parlor and did something I'd never done in the four years I'd known her. I checked her phone.

What I saw broke me. Tamia was sleeping with her boss. I saw that he continually invited her to his house after work, and not once, NOT ONCE, did she say, "We shouldn't be doing this" or "I have a husband, Tom." Tom—that was his name—the tall, handsome man whose hand I had shaken and spoken to briefly at one of their company parties. Tom, who I thought hugged my wife too long and stared at her backside too long; Tom, who I thought made too much eye contact with Tamia during his speech. I told myself she was a company favorite and how lucky I was to have her. "For Tamia." When she woke up, I was standing beside the bed and looking at her. I shoved her phone in her face and asked, "Why?" She started crying and told me how Tom had hit on her from the first day she was employed at the company and was remarkably resilient in his advances. She told me he refused to stop even after she was married.

"What are you saying?" I stopped her. "Wh-What do you mean even after you were married?" She kept crying and said they were having sexual relations the whole time. When I met her, I dated her for two years. I asked for her hand in marriage with that diamond ring—the diamond ring that caused her mother to pull a Judas on her, which caused her father to bellow, which threw everybody into a laughing fit. She told me Jennifer was not mine. Jennifer, my daughter, was actually Tom's. My hands were shaking; it was a shocking revelation. "Are you crazy?!" I screamed in anger.

I threw on a pair of clothes and marched to the car. I blindly drove off in the direction of her office. The car screeched to a stop at the front, and I went into the office and up the stairs. I said a few cursory "good mornings" and walked like an insane man to Tom's office. He saw me through his glass doors. "Hey, buddy! Come in!" I came in and went straight for his face. I smashed his laptop and threw a few more punches before I was picked up from behind and thrown outside his office and eventually outside the building. He stood at the entrance and smirked. "You throw a nasty punch. I won't be pressing charges." I picked myself up and drove home. A week later, I filed for divorce. I received a lot of calls from her, sniffling and crying remorsefully. I heard it all in the many voicemails she left. When I got tired of it, I started blocking her calls. Tamia broke me. I didn't understand how I would continue my life.

The divorce case was settled, and she gained full custody of both kids. I fought fiercely against it, but it was of no use. I was hurt, and I honestly was in no shape to be a parent. I was in my own head and dealing with what seemed to be the worst pain ever. I started drinking a lot. I couldn't bear the pain. Every morning I woke up hardly able to move. I would start my day with alcohol before dragging myself to work. Life was useless. Everything was useless. Over the next few months, I became a person even I did not recognize.

Despite the DNA test confirming Jennifer was not my baby, I knew that I wanted to be in her life. The time spent with her was so special to me, and I was not ready to give that up. Gary, the son I got to be with, was neglected. I constantly forgot to pick him up after school, and a kind parent or teacher would drop him off eventually. I left him alone most days and gave him money to buy his food. The only thing I had going for me was work, but I began to slack off there too. I staggered into work later and later every day and spent my time sleeping. It started with the bonus cuts, and then it was the salary slashes because my efficiency was declining. One day, I arrived at work at noon to see a letter on my desk saying I shouldn't bother coming to work the next day… or ever again. I was fired.

While driving home, I looked at myself in the rearview mirror. I was finished. There was nothing to live for anymore. I heard a loud horn and looked back at the road, too late. BOOM! I ran off the road slamming right into a large tree. That pretty little Camaro that Tamia loved was now scrap metal, and I was there clinging on to my life. Everything went black. All I remember was the loud boom and waking up in the hospital (a few days later, according to my nurse). I was severely injured and spent a month in the hospital. It was the worst month of my life. I was dealing with heartbreak, physical pain in my body, and now mental disarray because someone literally had to feed me and help me use the restroom. After I was discharged from the hospital, I went home. The only problem was I did not have a home at the time. I gave Tamia the house in the divorce. I wanted my kids to have somewhere to stay. So, despite the infidelity, I did not put up a fight and simply asked for a quick way out. I had been staying in raggedy motels and with friends when I could. However, after a stern and embarrassing talk with my mother, I decided to move back home.

I packed all my belongings and moved back home to live with my parents. Just great! I'm a grown man who just lost his family, job, and car, and now here goes my dignity. I needed a way out. I needed fixing. That was when I reached out for help. Jimbo, a good friend of mine, had a bit of a drinking problem. He was taking the necessary steps to get himself clean. Jimbo recommended I join him at group therapy. I wasn't thrilled about going, but at this point, what else did I have to lose? I began going to group therapy meetings. I attended the group therapy sessions at the Community Center, sponsored by the local church. There I met this woman, Bridget. She was nice to me, and we became friends. I shielded myself from anything more profound. I didn't want to be hurt again. I kept going to the group meetings and talking to her more and more. Eventually, she confided in me that she'd gone through a similar experience with her ex-husband.

I was surprised, wondering how someone as beautiful as this woman could be hurt like that. It also felt good to finally know that there was someone who understood my pain. I told her what had happened to me. She cried with me as she hugged me. She gave me a Bible to read and verses to meditate on daily. She told me it helped her. I followed her advice, and my wounds began to heal. I started applying for jobs again just before my savings were exhausted. I began to take care of myself once more. I felt wholesome. I felt good. Meanwhile, Bridget and I were getting closer and closer, speaking to each other more and understanding ourselves. This was nothing like the fast-paced relationship I had with Tamia; we took time to understand each other.

In Isaiah 41:10, God says: "So do not fear, for I am with you; do not be dismayed, for I am your God. I will strengthen you and help you; I will uphold you with my righteous right hand." God's love strengthened and lifted me during those difficult times. I began each day by reading and meditating on Bible verses Bridget had given me. Slowly but surely, God restored my soul; I was healed again. After a few years of friendship and dating, I married Bridget. We had a small intimate wedding. The pastor and a couple of witnesses were all that were present. We got married and have been happily married ever since. We pray together and serve God together. I began to mend my relationship with my son and eventually my daughter as well. I was the only father she knew, and I was determined to be a good father, blood or not. God also added to our family with a set of twins for Bridget and me. We named them Harmony and Hope.

This was the peace God had given me and the hope for tomorrow through his healing. My old job hired me back, and after a year of solid work, I was promoted to a higher position. I'm writing to you, my friend, to tell you God can men your broken heart. God can restore everything that you thought you lost. I'm whole again, and I feel great. Tamia and I are working together as co-parents. It's not always easy, and we disagree on parenting styles, but we are making it work. Bridget is an amazing wife and mother. Despite her job, she still takes care of home. I make sure I'm doing my part to take care of her as well. We have an open line of communication. She makes me feel loved and never neglected like before. I understand now that I had to endure the pain and agony to get to this place of peace I am experiencing.

I am not saying everything is all rainbows and sunshine because it's not. Marriages require hard work to sustain. It takes two people choosing each other EVERY day. Tamia hurt me to my core. She embarrassed me and made me feel like nothing. However, I'm here today saying thank you. Had she never done what she did, I would have never experienced what real love was supposed to feel like. In the hospital, I prayed over and over for a heart that forgives. I did not want to hold grudges against her or against my kids. Thanks to God, despite all that happened, I have respect for her as the mother of my kids, and I honor her for the woman she is striving to be each day. Therapy really helped me work through my anger and resentment. I'm happy Jimbo convinced me to go to those therapy sessions.

I share this story with you because I want to be the Jimbo in your life. If you need restoration or to find peace, there is help. Go see a therapist, your pastor, or a friend—whatever it takes to get that peace restored in your life. Stay in the fight. God has you in his hands.

God's Love Lifted Me

I was born into a broken family. My father was an alcoholic who always beat my mother. He left and came back every weekend to sleep in the house. By Monday, the house was void of him, and my mom had a black eye. This continued until one Friday evening. This particular night, he walked in to meet four hefty men. They beat him senselessly and dumped him outside the house.

You'd think my mother would have given me the love I lacked. She beat me for every little thing I did, no matter how minor. If I slept late, my mother slapped me. If I was slow, my mother smacked me. My mother beat me for everything. My siblings, all boys, didn't help matters. They kept mute. As the girl of the house, I took all the blame. I needed to escape and quickly. I was pretty, and all the boys told me so. Only a few were courageous enough to say it to my face, the others through indecent stares and swinging hands. I detested this attraction at first until I went home every night. I realized that it was the only positive praise I'd ever get between my life circle of home and school. So, I began talking to Jason, one of the boys in the mix of courageous and indecent stares. He was sweet and listened to me.

One night, a few weeks after we started talking, he slipped his hand under my skirt and up my thigh. I didn't move. He took it higher, and I slapped his arm down. He smiled and tried again. This time, when I slapped his hand, he told me to behave my age. I whimpered, and he promised to hit me if I screamed. We were alone at his place after school, and I couldn't do anything. He had his way with me and had sex with me. I cried and cried. He told me to keep quiet and called me ugly. He told me I wasn't that pretty anyway, and he just needed my attention. Then he kicked me out. I couldn't talk to anyone. I couldn't speak to my mother. She would beat me and call me a "good-for-nothing slut" the same way she had when I wasn't even talking to boys. I couldn't speak to any of the girls in school. So, I kept it to myself, wondering why this had happened to me. I concluded I wasn't beautiful after all, and I deserved the way my mother, my brothers, and Jason had treated me. The walls of my mind were the only thing holding my self-esteem. When they broke, I broke too.

I hated myself, and I didn't understand why. No one loved me, and I just didn't get it. So, I let loose and spread my legs for every Tom, Dick, and Harry. No kidding—there was a Tom, Dick, and Harry. I went wild. I was 14 years old. By the age of 15, I had been touched inappropriately by every boy in my class, and I was the topic of discussion every Friday afternoon by the girls with their hushed voices and accusing glances. My self-esteem was in hell. I entered college, and it was worse. I attempted to keep myself clean from the onset, but the compliments toward me by the boys boosted how I felt about myself. A year in, I started having sex again. Boys would approach me and shower me with compliments, and within a week, we would have sex. The first year, it was about four boys. The following year, I decided to stick to one person as if what I had done in past years would evaporate. It started great with Jackson, and he took care of me. I thought that I was in love. It was beautiful. He bought me gifts often, was a good listener, and was what I considered a proper boyfriend. But it didn't last. We were six months in when he met someone I was intimate with back in high school. It turned out they were long-time friends as well. He spent the night out with him.

When I met him the next day, he was a different person. He ignored what I said and was quiet most of the time, looking at me like I was a strange person. I begged him to talk to me. Eventually, when he spoke, he told me that he and his friend had a little chat. He said he knew of my past and couldn't believe I had lied to him for so long. Then, he told me it was over. I stared at him and kept staring as he stood to walk away.

In the days that followed, I cried my eyes out. I felt like I would die and spent hours under the shower, trying to wash the dirt off my body. Why was I so unloved? I didn't understand. I didn't date or have sexual relations with anybody again until after I had left college and started working.

Some months into working for a huge corporation, one of the executives, Victor, approached me, and we started talking. He was sort of cute and very rich, but I was more interested in the wealth of stories he always had about one experience or another. We spent our lunch breaks together, and soon, we were the talk of the office. He would spend inappropriate hours in my office, and it was exciting—more exciting than anything I'd experienced in my life. What made it fabulous was the fact that we would just talk and do nothing else—talk, eat, go on walks, go to the park—just talk.

One day, he called and told me he was leaving the company and relocating to another part of the country. I asked why. He was silent, and then I heard the harsh sounds of the dial tone resound in my ear. I frantically called him again and again. Victor never picked up. The next day, I got to the office and waited all day for one of his visits, but none came. I stared at the door, my heart pounding until I couldn't take it anymore. I took the elevator to the executive floor.

His door opened quite easily, but the office was empty. I just looked with tears brimming in my eyes. I got into my car and went home. It had happened again. I kept asking myself what was wrong with me.

How could a couple of mistakes I made when I was young keep affecting me? I had cut contact with everybody I schooled with. I no longer spoke to my mother or brothers. I did my best to keep everyone from the past out of my life. I tried to turn over a new leaf. Nothing worked. I wondered if my life was over. I wondered if I could simply scrub out my past. I picked up a pamphlet on my way back from work; those energetic Christians shared them every day with smiling faces. I read it that night with sleepy eyes and made a mental note to attend the church at the address on the back. On Sunday, I shuffled my feet into a congregation of happy, dancing people. I wondered what made these people so vibrant, so energetic. What was the source of their joy? I joined regardless; I had nothing to lose.

I felt myself filling up with such joy as I danced all my pain away. I shook my body energetically, just like I saw the people do, and raised my voice even louder than they did. I realized I'd been looking for love all this while to fill the emptiness inside me from my childhood. There'd been an emptiness I'd tried to fill with my sexual promiscuity, which didn't suffice when I'd tried to feel my family's love by serving them only to get insulted. That emptiness, that hole, was now being filled up with the love of God. I was overjoyed. I went for the altar call and gave my number to the pastor. Since that day, God has turned my life around. I stopped thinking about Victor, who'd refused to contact me since he left mysteriously. I spent all night reading my Bible and praising God. I was more complete than I'd ever been.

About a month later, I got a phone call from an unknown number. I picked it up and recognized Victor's voice. I almost fell from my seat with excitement. The first thing I did was to ask what his problem was. He kept apologizing profusely and told me he'd narrate everything at lunch. When we met for lunch, he told me he'd shown my picture to some of his friends, and he'd gotten an adverse reaction. They'd told him about my former life, and he was scared he was wasting his time with me because I would eventually cheat. I just shook my head and told him I hadn't been that person for more than ten years, and I didn't see why I would do that to him. I sighed and told him to leave if he wanted to. He didn't. Victor knelt and told me he was willing to make it work now. He'd gotten an impression in his heart for the past week telling him to find me, and he finally did. He said he wasn't willing to let me go this time.

We've been married for three years now, and it has been amazing. I'm glad I found God and got rid of the hole within me. Victor and I read the Bible and pray together every day. God cleared my past and all of my sins were washed away. It doesn't matter what others say about you; what God says, is what matters! While many people talked about me, it wasn't until I went to that church service that someone actually tried to help me. I remember the choir singing, *"Love Lifted Me."* People used my past to count me out and throw me away, but God used my past to show me my purpose. My past prepared me to realize that I may desire a lot of things, but with God, I have everything.

Psalm 27:1 says, "I will lift my eyes to the hill, from whence cometh my help." If you are discouraged and it seems as though things are not working out for you, remember the promises of God. He has promised you that you will drink from the rivers of milk, and if He has said it, you will because He never reneges. Keep serving Him because nothing else will fill that hole inside of you except Him. Not drugs, not men, nothing on this earth can do it. Only God can, and believe me, if He did it for me, then He can do it for you.

Where's My Husband

Growing up, my friends teased me with names such as "wifey." This started around the age of 14. Puberty had taken control and blessed me with a body I had no idea what to do with. It earned me longer-than-appropriate glances from men old enough to be my father and drooling stares from boys my age. I liked the attention a bit, but deep down, I really didn't want it. I was raised in a strict Christian home. We held devotion together every morning and attended church on Sundays, unlike most kids my age. I learned how to pray at a very early age. I took it so seriously—more than my siblings. At the age of 16, I even started attending Wednesday night Bible study and Friday night services. I tried to keep my focus on things my parents taught me were right.

I didn't participate in any of the beauty pageants in school. I knew I was beautiful. I didn't need any competition to tell me that. I also didn't join because I heard some of the things that went on in the background—that the girls sometimes did dirty things in order to progress in the competition, and I couldn't stain myself like that. My body was and still is, a temple of the Holy Spirit. I put my head down and worked hard, ignoring boys and many extracurricular activities. Whenever I let loose a little bit, the entire class was excited—I brought the vibes. I had my guard up still and wouldn't accept alcohol or drugs. As I grew older, I allowed myself to be wooed by a few boys before I graduated, but I made sure I didn't do anything that defiled me. I'm telling you this part because I'm human, and we have our limits. I serve God with all my heart, but I told myself a little of this and that couldn't hurt. As long as I kept true to my promise to God, and I was sure I wasn't committing any sin.

My dedication to my schoolwork paid off, and I was admitted to Yale on scholarship after scoring through the roof on my SATs and achieving insanely high scores on all other tests. Paying attention to God, family, and my education paid dividends. I began praying and talking to God even more and joined all the prayer groups on campus. My relationship with God grew more profound, and I started to understand things I never had before. I devoured my books with a hunger I didn't even understand. I spent most of my time in the library.

I breezed through college, graduating with first-class honors in business management. I picked up numerous awards as an entrepreneur and was even given a grant to go to Harvard Business School after that. I was on cloud nine. I did it all by being close to God. Things came more effortlessly for me than they did for other people, even though I had already worked harder than most. Having the grace of God in your life means you freely receive things you often don't deserve. You get about ten times your effort in rewards for serving God. You may work harder, or you may not, but the results multiply when you follow God. This is the principle I've been thriving on throughout my life.

I finished Harvard Business School and made my way into the business sector of America. With guidance and under the mentorship of renowned leaders, I launched a company. I put all my energy into it and watched the fruits of my labor grow. As my company grew, I suddenly noticed I unintentionally cut off men. After my run of relationships in high school, I had a declining rate of men approaching me. I scared most of them off with a tight schedule, excuses, and sometimes, I was just plain rude. As I reflected on it, I concluded I was doing what was best for me. I could have time for men later, but not then. But that wasn't the case. It was one thing to think about it and another thing to actually do it. I was young then—32 years old—and I wanted to achieve my goals. I spent all my time ensuring my company was growing and reaching new heights. And it did. I was now 37, beautiful, and successful. I decided to loosen up for good and have some fun. I started going places other than my office. I met a man, and we began talking. His name was Jerry, and he owned the bar where we first met. We had one, two, three dates, and I never heard from him again.

I met another man, Ben. We went out for dinner and got to talking about our careers and work life. It was weird when I mentioned my accomplishments. He got up with a grunt, saying I was too proud, and talked like a peacock. That was just one of them. There were many more.

All the men I met shied away from me—half because of my career accomplishments, the other half I still don't know why till today. I spent a lot of time looking in the mirror, admiring my face and body, and then wondering why was I not enough? What was missing? When I turned 40, I stopped mentioning my age during dates. The times I said it, I never saw the man again. Even as I stopped, I couldn't hide it on my skin. As beautiful as I was, age was beginning to take its toll on me. The number of men that approached me declined, and so did my confidence. I wondered if I was destined to die alone.

I wanted a family, a baby, something to live for. No matter how huge it was, my company was still perishable and not someone I could talk to. I wanted companionship. It seemed as though I was getting too old for that. If my career accomplishments didn't scare away the men, my age did. It was baffling how quickly men who wanted a woman of their standard moved away so quickly when they met one. I turned to God. I prayed my heart out and listed marriage and children as my top prayer points consistently, month after month, year after year. The same things kept happening. I cried to God in the dark and in the light. The same things happened nonetheless.

Year after year, it was a mental war for me. I carried myself every day to work, feeling dread that I would never bear or nurture a family. I would never have children to call my own. I would die a haggard old woman and a wealthy old bird. My parents began to call and pile the pressure on me. "We aren't getting any younger, baby," they would say and giggle to themselves over the phone, but I heard the underlying pain. I listened to the resentment of "You're our only child. We want a grandson, not money. We want a continuation of our blood." I never told them, but these words messed up my mental state so much that I started cutting their calls while they were speaking, unable to take any more of it.

My mom came to visit and asked me gently what the matter was. I broke down and narrated how miserable I had been for the past three years, no companionship, no partner, no child. My mom cradled me in her arms and told me it was okay. She told me God's time was the best, and He was probably preparing me for something bigger. I underwent three years of torture. I didn't understand. I was 40, as beautiful as ever, and successful but no husband and no child. Was I meant to believe it was some sort of test for something better? I couldn't. I wouldn't. I began withdrawing from God, slowly but surely. I prayed less, read my Bible less, and attended church less. My phone constantly rang—calls from my pastor and concerned church members—and I allowed everyone to go to voicemail. I didn't want to seem pathetic and bother the church with my issues. I was a bit sure there were already questions and talk about my situation. The successful lady got older and still hadn't waltzed into a Sunday service on a man's arm yet. The beautiful lady who sang her heart out on the weekends yet had nothing to show for it. I didn't want to experience it in real time. You might say I was overreacting or that I didn't need a man to make me happy. Let me tell you, I was lonely with nothing to show but years of dedication put into my business and education. There was everything to show for that commitment but nothing to show for my womanhood. No man was in sight that was willing to make a commitment to me.

At age 41, I tanked. After giving temporary ownership of the company to my partner, I vanished. I stayed in my house 24/7, watching Netflix and eating. It felt like I was unwinding my entire life. I was accustomed to staying so focused all the time. I allowed myself to be accessible for a bit way back in high school, but never since then. I reasoned I had nothing to lose, but there was a limit to the time in which I could go AWOL. The company I worked so hard to build could slip away from my eyes in the blink of an eye. It was on one of those sulking days I got a knock on my door. It was my pastor. He'd come to try to save me from myself (as he put it). I let him in reluctantly, and he came into my living room, looking at me in bewilderment. "Where is the vibrant woman I've known all these years?" I told him I didn't understand God's concept of time or what it meant for me. Was I to suffer because I knew and served Him? Was this his way of paying me back for all the years I did not keep my body as a temple? I would ask God often, "where is my husband?"

My pastor smiled and told me, "God's ways are not the ways of man. I won't understand them, and you won't. All I can tell you is to trust Him. You mentioned you trusted and served Him all these years, and it paid you dividends. Why don't you think it would still pay now? Besides, I can feel your blessing is close. Why pull away from Him now? Matthew 7:33 'But seek ye first the kingdom of God and all things will be added to you.' All things. Not some things. Go back to God and ask Him. You will receive."

I cried and cried and knelt for him to pray for me. The next day, I cleaned up my house and went to God in prayer—heartfelt, earnest prayer from the depths of my soul. I told Him I would keep serving Him and whatever He wanted to do, and at whatever time, was good with me. Five years later, I was married to a husband I never believed existed. He bought my company ultimately, putting ownership in our name, telling me it was time to rest when I told him my story. We have two chubby boys (we adopted) in their teens, and I've never been more grateful.

I still have ownership and control of my company; I'm just not the one running the day-to-day activities. It's growing steadily and paying me heavily. I have a kind, empathetic husband and kids in the upbringing of the Lord. I would have never pictured my life like this. Even though I never imagined adoption as my way to motherhood, it has been the most rewarding experience ever. At almost 50 years old, God's promise to me came true. I am so glad His way was better than my way. It was so worth the wait. The only thing worse than waiting on God is wishing you had. I'm glad I can say that I waited on God; for His time is always the best. The Bible says in Isaiah 40:31, "But they that wait upon the Lord shall renew their strength; they shall mount up with wings as eagles; they shall run, and not be weary; and they shall walk, and not faint." Remember, serving God pays dividends. I'm still reaping those dividends in every way.

I Never Gave Up

It's tough accepting God's timing. I would state that waiting on God is one of the hardest things in the world to do. As Christians, we know that God does not operate according to our time. My grandma would always say, "He may not come when you want Him, but He's always on time." If you are anything like me, then you too have probably become frustrated in the waiting room of life. You know what God said. You know what He promised, but it seems like He is taking forever to deliver on what He said. Follow me as I take you on this decade-long journey of waiting on God to bless us with a child.

For ten years, I waited on God to bless my husband and me with children. It was debilitating, humiliating, and mentally crushing. Year after year, day after day, I was praying and crying out to God to bring forth children. At age 25, I married the man of my dreams. We started a great life together, looked out for each other, and decided not to have babies too fast. Nick and I took the first two years of our married life to elongate our honeymoon and enjoy the intimacy of being newlyweds. That was before the "baby crazies" started. That was what my friend Judith and her husband referred to it as, during our double date a month after our wedding. I watched Judith constantly interrupted by her crying baby as she tried to rock him to sleep or silence him. It dulled the atmosphere. Even though babies are cute, on a two-hour date, the cuteness dissipates after about 15 minutes if the baby is constantly crying and gasping. I panicked and pulled on Nick's shirt the entire date. When we got in the car, I told him I wasn't ready to have babies yet. He laughed and said he was okay with waiting. We had the conversation and decided on two years of avoiding the baby crazies.

We began our married lives and basked in each other's love. It was a good time. We had dates, dinners, eat-ins, gifts, and all sorts of corny and cheesy things during that time. It seemed our honeymoon phase would actually last for two years, and I was enjoying every minute of it. After two years, we discussed having children. It seems we both were ready and finally okay with starting a family. I knew this would make my parents happy. During my parents' numerous visits, they always asked where their grandchildren were or when we were going to start having them. Nick and I explained our plans to them every time, but it fell on deaf ears. Every holiday they would ask me again like they wanted me to feel what I was doing to them. My dad would hold his chest and pretend to topple backward, telling me I was wielding a sharp sword and had passed it through him. We decided it was time to remove the sword from dad's heart and work on having children, also giving my parents what they desired.

Halfway through our fourth year of marriage, it became painfully apparent that our honeymoon phase was over. Nick and I began to drift apart because of work and other things I couldn't explain at the time. We spoke less at home and went straight to bed after dinner. I didn't understand what was happening, but I did nothing to stop it. We did nothing to stop it.

One night after dinner, he said, "We should work on that baby. "I replied with a smirk on my face, "We should start trying." We had not made love in a while. We both decided that we would be more intentional and more intimate with each other. After all, you can't make a baby without trying, right? Well, we tried, and we tried. I admit I really enjoyed all the trying, but I was a little hurt by the result. Nevertheless, we kept right on trying.

And we did for nine years. The first year, nothing happened. I took it as expected. It was our first year trying. Some couples didn't have kids until after two years of marriage without contraceptives. Some didn't after three years. So, I felt good about it. There couldn't be any problems at this point, could there be? Nick considered seeing a doctor, but I scolded him for such a thought. What if he was the impotent one? I laughed, but he went inside our bedroom with a grim face. I saw him smiling when I came in. Sex was loosening us up a bit with the intimacy. If we wanted a baby, it was a necessary evil.

The second year, I got pregnant, bringing sighs of relief from both of us. It was as if I knew I was a bit rusty in the first year. I told Nick this jokingly, and he laughed too. We loosened up even more, waiting for our unborn child. The marriage was better, and the unspoken tension was much easier now. We talked more again, slowly drifting back to who we were before we went apart. The necessary evil was helping. We showed off my small belly to our friends and family. My dad smiled and put his hand on his chest as if to remove something lodged there—funny old man. I didn't try to hide it at work. Babies—born and unborn—were for flaunting, and I was going to take every leave I could get.

I woke up one night, four months into the pregnancy, feeling something between my legs. My period couldn't be here. I shuffled to the bathroom to check the problem. I looked to see a steady flow of blood out of my body. At the same time, I felt a sharp pain in my back, and I screamed before passing out. I awoke in a hospital bed with no baby bump, no bulge, and my best friend Judith standing over me with wet, sad eyes. My husband was sitting in the corner with his head down. The doctor walked in, shaking his head at a bunch of papers in his hands. I had miscarried.

I cried for a long time. I wouldn't talk to my husband or any of my friends. I didn't understand. It was internally shattering. I began to really connect with the baby at three months, and at four months, I miscarried. In the third year, we tried to have a baby, but it was a failure. I didn't get pregnant. We went to the doctor without anyone telling us. The doctor ran tests on me and Nick but didn't find anything wrong with us. "Nothing out of the ordinary," he told us with our butts in the plush chairs of the office. We entered year four of trying, and the result was the same as the year before. I read more articles, studied my cycles, and we even only had sex when I was ovulating. Nonetheless, nothing happened. We visited a different doctor, did more tests, and got the same answer. "Nothing out of the ordinary." This time the office chairs were wooden and not so soft on our bottoms.

In the fifth year, I got pregnant twice and miscarried twice. The first time, I was three and a half months in and riding the bus back home. It was a cool day, but I noticed my body heating up. I passed out just when it reached my stop, and I woke up in another hospital bed with my husband pacing up and down. Finally, he came to hold me and whispered in my ear that the baby was gone. I went hysterical, screaming, "What do you mean 'gone!'" The doctor pleaded with me to calm down, and my husband put his weight on me to avoid ripping my drip out of my arm. He kept speaking calmly into my ear, but it wasn't helping. I kept thrashing around and got out of his grip. I ran downstairs. The nurse found me in the reception area staring at the TV, sober, with tears flowing down my cheeks. She took me by the hand gently and led me back to my room. My husband kissed me goodbye when I told him I wanted to be alone. That night, I cried myself to sleep.

The second time that year, it was the same as the first. Nick rushed me to the hospital as I dozed off. I woke to see the doctor shaking his head. My husband was in the corner, looking at me with a sad face. Judith was in the hospital with her husband, her big round eyes and cheeks tear-stained. I looked around and said nothing, going back to sleep. I had miscarried again. Year six. Year seven. Year eight. Two more miscarriages. My dad came to comfort me, but his hand remained on his chest. I had stabbed him with my imaginary sword, but it wasn't remotely funny to me anymore. My mother just sat and cried with me all the time, like she had felt all five miscarriages too. Their empathy didn't help the fact that my relatives started to talk and formulate stories around my barrenness. Some said I had committed unforgivable sins in the past, and a cousin asked me to beg God for forgiveness. I looked at her in bewilderment. But then, I overheard an uncle tell my mother I was reaping the fruits of promiscuity and premarital sex. God knows I was confused. Nick and I grew closer and closer during this period. I sometimes shied away from him, scared that my inability to give him children would affect our relationship. It didn't. He apologized for drifting from me earlier in our marriage and told me—child or no child—he would never leave me. He accepted my flaws for what they were, and we only talked about the miscarriages when I brought them up to vent. He dismissed my fears and told me it was simply a moment in time that we would get through together. We hardly talked about it still, avoiding the subject like the plague. We focused on finding more meaningful things about ourselves and our marriage to work on. I think we wouldn't be where we were without that trial period in which we chose to stick together and understand each other even more.

Year nine, no child. The following year, almost casually—since no one expected anything spectacular from my pregnancies anymore—I gave birth. My husband made me hide the pregnancy the entire term to avoid the sympathies and questions we had gotten the past five times. Nobody knew—not Judith, not my parents. I couldn't help crying and touching the baby all over to see if he was real. Nick couldn't help it either; he was thrilled. When we eventually announced it, there was disbelief across the board and then a wild celebration. Our house turned into a constant mini-event center, with different groups of people making their way over to congratulate us week in and week out, so there was always some form of food available. My parents' visits were special; my father's hands spread out wide to hug me, and my mother knelt to thank God—I only managed to hold her from lying down. We dedicated the child to the Lord and gave our testimony. It was mind-blowing for the audience, and we couldn't even contain all the congratulations and compliments. Radio and TV stations across the nation broadcasted and played a recording of it over and over again. After the spy in the Bible, we named our son Joshua, who was bold enough to advance into giants' territory and defeat them even after being discouraged by some of his team. It was what we wanted him to be: fearless in the face of opposition, intelligent, cunning, and a victor. He was born from pain; however, he would thrive amid that pain. When the going gets tough, God gets going.

If you're in a place where you feel what you deserve is being withheld, keep trusting God, even when it's not the easiest thing to do. It's never easy to pass through these tribulations. You may have mentally stripped yourself of your self-worth after a prolonged test like the one I passed through. Nonetheless, remember you're stronger than you think. You are better than you think. You have inherent capabilities you don't even know of yet. I believe in you. Trust in the Lord always. He will always be there for you. Don't give up on God, and he won't give up on you.

Just Say No, But I didn't

When people see who I am today, they never remember that I walked around a tainted man for almost half my life. I've gone through a lot, but with help, it doesn't show as badly now. Given where I grew up, it was almost impossible to avoid social vices. As a kid, I was hitting a few cigarettes a week with some of the men on my street. They welcomed me every time I came to sit with them as these guys discussed adult matters. I snuck a pack away at the end of every week, and once in a while, I would hide in the basement and light one up.

My friends introduced me to more complex things as a teenager: cocaine, heroin, and weed. I wouldn't take the cocaine or heroin at first but stayed stuck with weed. I even became a mini-distributor, selling weed to junkie teenagers and high schoolers for quick cash. Eventually, I was over weed, and I needed something more substantial. I needed cocaine. I remember the drug campaigns at school, "Just Say No," but I didn't. I rejected heroin, saying I wasn't quite ready to plunge needles into myself, and I was happy to save it for another day. I was 22 years old at this point, a dropout with no direction in life, just sitting around all day, smoking and selling drugs. Cocaine sold faster than weed and brought in more cash, but that meant I became mixed up with the wrong crowd. Don't get me wrong; I was already in quite the bad crowd. Selling cocaine put me in another league. I dealt with bigger shot-callers who were way more dangerous. Usually, I was able to get my weed from local suppliers, but cocaine was a totally different ball game. I worked for a guy, who worked for a guy, who worked for cartels. I'm not sure how I got myself into this, but honestly, I loved every second of it. I drove a new Range Rover, had a fly condo, and spent money recklessly. I was living the high life, literally and figuratively.

Most of my customers were dreadfully skinny, some bulging at the arms with eyes sunken in so far—their skeletal structures showing on one part of the body or another. I didn't mind as long as the money came in. I did not care about anybody but myself. All I wanted was to make a dollar and get my fix. I just sold and smoked, smoked and sold. Well, that was the problem my friends. As the old saying goes, "Don't get high on your own supply!" I was smoking just as much as I was selling. The money I made was mostly used to get high. One fateful Saturday, I decided to go out for some beers. It was a no- business day for me, a much-needed break. Normally in this business, we didn't get breaks, but I decided I was going to take a day for myself. Considering that I was high as an astronaut, I should've stayed home. But I thought, "Whatever!" It was football Saturday, and I wanted chicken & beer. Someone else sat beside me at the bar, shifting my outstretched leg. I stared at him furiously and put my leg back. He moved it again. I remember telling him he could ask me to move nicely if he wanted to sit. We exchanged a few words and were escorted out by the security guards. When we got outside, I headed for my car. I knew the last thing I wanted was for the police to be called because I had a little "coke" in the truck. As I was making my way to the truck, I remembered something crashing across my head. It was a beer bottle buddy picked up outside the bar. Before I knew it, we were exchanging punches. I was high, and he was very drunk. We fought for what seemed to be about 30 minutes. It got out into the road. The next thing I knew, I was atop him, swinging and hitting him harder and harder. By the time they pulled me off, the police were there. The people around called an ambulance. He had no pulse. I began to reason that maybe I had taken too much cocaine. The young man who I was fighting with died right on the scene. We were both intoxicated. My life flashed before my eyes as I was arrested and hauled off in the cruiser.

It didn't take long for a jury to find me guilty. There was nobody to bail me out, or at least nobody that wanted to. In court, I was sentenced to 20 years for manslaughter/possession. I was 23. My lawyer fought as a self-defense case but failed. My ties to the drug world did not help. It seemed as though the police were already watching me and waiting for their opportunity to get me off of the streets. I will admit, I cried because I knew that my life would never be the same. All the women, fancy cars, nice home, and name-brand clothes were all about to vanish because of one stupid argument. If that wasn't bad enough, state prison was a nightmare.

It had some of the meanest, nastiest people I had ever seen. However, I mixed in easily, moving with the big dawgs, unlike the other newcomers who'd huddle and make for easy prey. I never got into a fight again, always being protected. I got used to being in prison, so much so that it almost felt like being at home. It seems that your street credits always follow you to prison. The man I ultimately worked for was right in prison with me. When he learned of my arrival, he wanted me to immediately begin working for him. The big men in jail were moving drugs and had a steady supply from the guards. I didn't have to sweat to see weed, meth, and cocaine. There was an unending supply. I reasoned, if I had 20 years of my life gone, why not waste it? So, I got high—all the time. I didn't go a day without shooting heroin into my veins with dirty, rusty needles or smoking crack. I was going through everything as fast as possible, and my body was becoming numb with every dose. I needed more potent stuff, and they gave me things that would knock me out for hours on end. It was beautifully horrible.

I got worse every year and transformed into a skinny and eye-sunken junkie. I was the very picture of an addict. I couldn't sleep without it. I couldn't go hours without touching some weed or meth. I would go into hysterics if I couldn't find my supply. It was bad. Year after year, I got thinner and thinner. Right before I was released, I got into a fight with one of my big bosses. He had accused me of stealing toilet tissue from him. While I know this seems funny, in prison, this is a real thing. I ended up with a broken tooth and a badly bruised body, which was more bone than flesh. So, I was ultimately thrown out of the cell. I was in new territory and without my supply.

 I experienced withdrawal symptoms while being beaten constantly. If not for the mercy of an inmate who helped me get water to handle the withdrawals, I would have died. I passed out for hours at a time, which was probably the only time I escaped from merciless beatings. I had been protected from these guys for the past 19 years, and now they had had their way with me. These inmates were serving life sentences, and so they held little or no regard for human life. The guards took me to another cell just to make sure I didn't pass on to glory. There, I lived the last year of my imprisonment in quiet, free from drugs, thanks to the hell of the previous year.

I was released a day before my 43rd birthday. I stepped out into the world, confused, and realized it had moved on without me. There were so many technological advancements and breakthroughs. Even without the new technology, there was a new order to things I did not understand. I tried to get a job during my first year out of prison, but it was futile as I ticked "ex-convict" on every employment form I filled out. This almost zeroed my chances of getting a job. Eventually, I managed to get a cleaning job to hold myself together, but after a few months, the company lost its contract, and the job was dissolved. The landlady threw the envelope in my face with a note that said, "Don't come back." So that was that. I had no money and no place to go. This led me to go back to living on the streets. I went to several job interviews. I would go to the local library and use the computers. This was a skill I picked up in prison.

Even the job interviews that were kind enough to ask me the nature of my crime veered away as fast as they came. It was discouraging. I wish I hadn't made that mistake 20 years ago. A friend, Michael, from way back, recognized me one day and stopped to help me. I was at my lowest. I was bones and clothes, dragging my feet on the road. I don't know how he recognized me; twenty years is a long time. Maybe the same way I recognized him.

He offered me a room in his apartment and promised me he would help me get back on my feet. I told him not to bother, that I was enough trouble to myself already. He was adamant, so I followed him. We got to a big duplex. I stared at it in awe. It was beautiful. I asked him what he did for a living, and he said, "While you were getting high, I was working." It stung a little, but I didn't mind. That was what happened. I thought I'd be up and, on my feet, once I moved in and started re-applying for jobs. Somehow, though, I couldn't motivate myself to do anything. I was just tired. I wanted to rest my body. I slept twelve hours a day and ate a lot. Michael didn't complain at first. I guess he understood what I had gone through. He gave me food all the time and made sure the kitchen and fridge were stacked. Slowly, I gained some weight back and looked like a human being once again. Some of my sanity was coming back. That was the worst part—understanding how to be free after 20 years in captivity.

After three months, he told me to get out of the house. I panicked, but he explained it was only during the day—I needed a job. So, I started applying and searching for jobs rigorously. It was no different from the last time. My convict status had seemingly stained me for life. I got denial after denial. I came back discouraged every time, and it was more complex and harder to apply. I'd applied to everything I was remotely qualified for. I got nothing.

I finished my GED in prison and took some business courses, which set me up to finish my Bachelor's degree in Business. For a regular person, not being able to provide for yourself means you go hungry and depressed. I was privileged not to experience the former, but I sank into myself. I answered the interviews with less confidence, which made no difference. Michael finally took pity on me and gave me an entry-level job with him. He was an entrepreneur and had started a few businesses, which was how he made his money. The only trade I ever knew was pharmaceuticals, I told him, and we laughed.

My new job was to organize and stack orders for new items before sending them out. Working at that level and being so close to Michael allowed me to understand the essential workings of the business. I listened in on some of his phone calls and saw how far he had spread his wings. For the first time in 15 years, I was genuinely motivated. I did my job with passion and so well that after a few weeks, he moved me up to take on something more complex. He kept moving me up until I was working directly with him. We eventually parted ways, but I did so with a wealth of knowledge. With the knowledge gained, I launched my own business. It was an easier start for me because of my experience and the things I had learned. In three years, I was making a serious profit and giving back to the community. I launched several businesses, some of them to give men just leaving prison a sense of direction. I knew it could be challenging and depressing outside prison walls; life seems to move on so fast without you. I'm glad that at least one person didn't write me off. With my past and my age, Michael didn't see an ex-convict like every other person did. He saw a man who could use some help, not more degrading talk. No matter what you've done, moving forward is hard when everybody knows what you did! While everyone thinks you're done and are no good, God always has a plan for you. God will never write you off as useless, despite what you've done in the past. Daniel 9:9, says "The Lord our God is merciful and forgiving, even though we have rebelled against Him." He can always see the potential in you and will make someone else see the same. He made Michael see the potential in me, and look at where I am today. Good friends are good for your health. Friends can help you celebrate good times and provide support during bad times. Friends prevent isolation and loneliness and give you a chance to offer needed companionship too. Friends can also increase your sense of belonging and purpose, boost your happiness, and reduce your stress. They can help improve your self-confidence or self-worth and help you cope with traumas, such as divorce, serious illness, job loss, or the death of a loved one. It was the faith of a friend that saved my life. I am thankful today that my friend gave me another chance at life.

The Fight of My Life

When my son's father tried to kill me, it made me rethink my entire life. I still don't know how I survived the situation. I'm just glad I came out alive. I made a promise to myself to protect my son and ensure he would never turn out like his dad. I made a lot of bad choices when I was younger, the majority involving men. I had been swayed by and attracted to flashy things since I was a kid—a fun activity then, but when puberty hit, it didn't turn out too well for me. It went from toys and plastic diamonds to men in big cars with shiny watches on their wrists. As I got older, I still followed the shiny wherever it went.

As a young girl at 19, with my mother's good looks, I always got the hoots and stares from men. I partied a lot with friends and had a few men come up to me every night. I didn't mind. I loved the attention. I gave out my number to the ones I deemed attractive, wealthy, or shiny enough. As I continued to mature naturally and mentally, coupled with the unending unsolicited advice from older women, I set my priorities right. However, not before I was involved with David. I met David on one of my girls' night out when I was 22. He looked clean, had a shaved head, one gold tooth, and a gleaming wristwatch. I instantly left my girls for him and followed him home that night. Not long after, I decided to take a break, permanently, from the promiscuous life. I had to finish school and focus on my career with a straight head. I was in deep with David. The relationship was good, even perfect the first year. David bought me a lot of things, spoiling me unnecessarily, and of course, I didn't mind.

I graduated from school and started my job search. David offered me the opportunity to stay at his place while I kept searching, and I obliged. I moved in with David a month after my graduation…bag and baggage. After two months, I realized it was a big mistake. Aside from the shiny and materialistic things, what attracted me to David was his assertiveness, aggressiveness, and unbending stance on almost everything. I considered it hot and sexy. As a young woman looking for a mating partner, those were standard qualities. Up close, although, it was scary. He was very touchy and got angry at the slightest aggravation, throwing things around the house and breaking them. He always had money to replace them, so I didn't complain about them breaking. I was just terrified of him.

He would always come back to apologize and say sweet things to me and buy me even more things. I always accepted his apology because how bad could it be? One day we argued, and he was raving around the house, smashing glass cups and bottles everywhere. I was so furious that I got up to shout back at him, and then I saw him rushing back to the room where I was. He looked like a possessed man, and he stunned me. Without hesitation, he lashed out at me. He began to choke me until I was lying there, nearly lifeless. I was confused. I thought he would never touch me. A few minutes later, he was at my feet, begging me not to leave him. At that moment, it was as if the world had stopped.

I forgave him, but that was the first attack of many. Even the little fights and arguments ended with red welts on my face and body. I threatened to leave him every time, and he would come begging. I knew I couldn't possibly leave him; he was paying for everything I was doing. I knew deep down I needed to go, and soon. I got pregnant again by David. I say again because, after two abortions he wanted me to have, I decided not to go through with it again. Unfortunately, he wasn't having it. He came to talk to me calmly about how he wasn't ready to be a father and did not need to shoulder that sort of responsibility. I simply responded, telling him I did not want to destroy my womb. He pleaded over and over, promising that was the last time. I denied his request and told him I chose myself.

Choosing me didn't sit well with David. He beat on me more often, slapping, punching, and kicking me. According to him, if I didn't want to remove it, he'd do it himself. I ran away from the house one Sunday afternoon to Anita, my best friend. She let me in and allowed me to sleep without fear. In the morning, she checked my body and was appalled by the bruises I'd sustained from past and recent beatings. I stayed in Anita's house for a while, slowly getting myself back together. She took care of me and ensured I was healing properly so my parents would not notice any scars when they came to see me. She helped me apply for and get a job when the pregnancy was not yet showing. I was grateful and couldn't possibly repay her for what she'd done for me.

I carried the child to full term and gave birth to a healthy baby boy. He was beautiful, and I loved him so much. He was adorable. Anita and I took turns taking care of him during my maternity leave, and when I started working, I hired a nanny. Everything was going well. Then I started receiving calls from David. He accused me of giving birth without his consent and running away with his son. I told him angrily that he rejected him, and I wasn't asking for his help, so what was the big deal? The last thing I heard was that he was going to stop at nothing to get custody. I panicked. I told the nanny to leave and carried my son everywhere with me. I lived in fear for weeks, and it was terrible. We installed alarms around the house, blinding lights on the driveway, and multiple baby monitors. For three weeks, there was nothing. We let down our guard and began to breathe more easily.

That was the mistake. One weekend I was home alone with my son. I heard the door opening and assumed it was Anita, naturally. The baby was in the bedroom, and I was in the living room with the baby monitor. The door opened, and I saw a ragged man whom I recognized as David come in. My heart flew into my mouth. I instinctively grabbed my phone and dialed Anita's number. It sent me straight to voicemail, and I said a single word: "Help!" Then he grabbed the phone and pounded on me.

He beat and bruised me terribly, then brought out a gun, pointing it at my head to shoot me. I was crying, begging, and pleading to do anything he asked. He didn't listen. He had the look of a madman in his eyes as he pointed the gun at me. As his finger tightened on the trigger, a bottle shattered on his head, and the gun fired, hitting the wall, and missed my head by inches. The gun hit the ground, and he was knocked out. From my face filled with tears, I could see Anita standing over me with a broken bottle in her hand and sobbing. The police arrived and asked me if I was pressing charges. I was about to say no, but Anita held my hands and said yes. She told me I'd been through enough. He was charged with counts of attempted murder, unlawful breaking and entering, and other things I couldn't wrap my head around. He was found guilty by the court and sentenced to two years in prison.

I spent a lot of my days living in fear and resentment. I feared that I and my son's life would forever be in danger. I held so much bitterness toward the man who mistreated me to the point he was ready to kill me. I was depressed for a long time and began to neglect my son, so I went to talk to a therapist. I found myself in the fight of my life.

The therapist suggested that I visit my ex and forgive him. I revolted and asked her to leave. What she was asking was simply unthinkable. But I kept deteriorating and eventually spoke about it with Anita. Anita agreed with my therapist that it was only for my good. So, a year after David was jailed, I visited him. I laid out the contents of my heart, sometimes raising my voice, sometimes speaking calmly. I ended by telling him I had no grudges against him and would not allow his irrationality and murderous personality to bother me anymore. I walked out of there a free person.

My son is seven years old now and has been under my parenting all this while. He has grown to be a healthy, lovely, and polite boy. I'm glad I decided to forgive and remove David entirely from my life back then. Had I held on to those grudges, I would have been resentful toward my son, who happens to really resemble David, his father. Ironically, David was brutally murdered while in prison. He got into a fight with an inmate and was stabbed to death. A part of me aches with pain for him, but another part feels that he got what he deserved. I know it may not be right to feel that way, but I realized that in life honestly, we need honesty. I needed to be honest with myself about everything and how my decisions played a major role in how things turned out. I also needed to be 100 percent honest pertaining to how I felt about David and our son. That's when I truly began to heal.

I'm finding happiness again. I am growing as a parent and doing the best I can for my son. I feel free, as I hold no grudges with anyone. I pray David found peace before leaving this earth. I spend my days now working and helping other women who are living like I was. You don't have to live like that. If you're mentally, verbally, or physically abused, I encourage you to find the strength to walk away. Find the Anita in your life to help you get freedom and peace. You deserve to be treated like a queen, and anything less is unacceptable.

Was It My Fault

My young ears were accustomed to every obscene word imaginable on the planet. My home was a battle arena of sorts, with my parents constantly fighting. I didn't cause the fights, but the ones that had me in the middle were on the crazy end of the spectrum. As a child, I was left thinking I was the cause of my parents' consistent fights, which made me feel terrible. My grades were affected, tanking badly. I would come home with bad grades, and another round of screaming and arguing would start, but not directed at me. It was always between my parents. Eventually, they couldn't handle each other anymore and started divorce proceedings.

They didn't know not to include me. Instead, they brought me to all the hearings and screamed more and more at each other. I was only ten years old then, and my parents had filled my head with their violent screams all the time, my mother crying, my father bellowing, and me in between. The proceedings went on and on for weeks, and they made sure I showed up for every single one, not bothering to give me food in the morning before dragging me out to fight for custody. They simply threw me in the car after each session and drove me back home, leaving me in an empty house with uncooked food. I tried to cook, but it ended in disaster many times. The result? More arguments and screaming, but again, they were not at me.

Despite the arguments not being aimed at me, I couldn't help but think, was it my fault. The judge presiding over their case granted the divorce but without custody to either of them. In his words, he "couldn't imagine leaving this promising child with either of you inconsiderate monsters." So, I went off to live with an aunt and continued school, in which I had fallen far behind. The last 13 years living with my parents left me scarred. I was confused and uninterested in everyone and everything. I became the kid who talked to no one, gliding in and out the school doors with my head always down. Everyone thought I was weird. I thought it was very cruel of the judge to remove me from my parents. They were crazy, but at least they were my parents. I didn't participate in any activity, sport, or club. I hated everything; it made no sense to me. When the heads of some organizations tried to convince me to join some activity or their community, I left them with either some obscene words or cold stares. Some of the girls went back crying, but I didn't care. They were all disgusting to me.

I didn't take care of my body anymore, apart from the courtesy of a shower. I would allow my hair to run wild all over my head and never used any form of deodorant or cologne. I just didn't care that much. I got worse and worse.

The only time I stayed more than two minutes in the shower was to hide the fact that I was crying. I would stay in the shower and cry for hours on end, scratching a razor over my body. I made a few cuts, drawing minimum blood. I wondered what I had done wrong to make everybody act this way toward me; my parents did not care enough to fight for me and kept arguing over what I had done. In my eyes, I was the cause of the divorce since they kept fighting whenever I did anything wrong. I was the entire problem with the marriage.

As I grew older, I considered suicide and started browsing suicide techniques. There were the traditional methods like hanging and various poisons—from the quickest to the most painful. My gallery and search bars were a mess, so I hid my phone from everyone. However, my aunt came across my unlocked phone once and saw everything. She was horrified and asked me what was wrong. I didn't say anything, so she put me in the car and drove me to school. She barged into the principal's office angrily, asking him why the students were bullying me. But of course, he'd had no such report, and he told my aunt as much. She insisted I was being picked on and showed him what she had found. His face took on a look of grave concern, and he asked me what was wrong.

I finally broke down and told them how my parents' divorce had wrecked me. I did not see purpose in life anymore. My aunt was crying too and consoled me, assuring me she'd make things better. She scheduled me for therapy the next week, every Friday after school. I didn't see any reason for it, and I was convinced it wasn't going to help me, so I skipped it. I came home with a big smile on my face every Friday, telling her therapy went well. This went on for some time, but I kept deteriorating.

I barely entered college, with terrible scores on everything. I was only accepted based on the story of my divorced parents. My aunt managed to slip this into every application I made. I wasn't helping matters, but my brain just wasn't interested in anything. My parents never called once after the divorce. They sent me monthly stipends as support but never called. They never checked up with my aunt to ask how I was doing. The only way I knew they were still alive was by overhearing my aunt's phone conversations. Otherwise, they could be dead for all I knew. The phone conversations my aunt was having convinced me they were alive, which drove me to ask more questions. Why didn't they call? Where were they? Etc..... I concluded they didn't care enough to call. I wasn't human enough to them. I was just an item, not a child, and more like a pet. It drove me crazy.

In my second year of college, I overdosed on lethal pills. I decided enough was enough and tried to take my life. My roommate came back early from class, and he found me foaming at the mouth on the floor. He raised the alarm, alerting the medical center. The ambulance picked me up and rushed to bring me back to life. I was almost gone, or so they said. But I made it. It was close, but I made it. When I woke up to the surprise of my overjoyed roommate, and a whole lot of other people, I was angry. I asked them who they thought they were to decide if I was to die or not. I was tired. Had they gone through even a fraction of what I had experienced? When I was discharged, I refused all visits and stormed back to my room on campus.

My roommate was awake, and I spilled insults and curses on him. He was confused and didn't say a word. He got up to leave, but before he did, he dropped a card on my bed. It was a therapist's card. The same therapist my aunt had been paying for nothing, ironically. I considered it, and since I had tried to leave this wretched earth and couldn't even be granted that, I visited her. When I told her my name, her eyes lit up. "You're the patient! You have about 50 paid sessions already. Come on, sit." The session started, and she paid more attention to me than anyone ever had. She asked probing questions, and I put up resistance initially, telling her only what I wanted her to know. However, she didn't let up; she was patient, smiling, and always taking notes like there was something she knew. I broke eventually and told her everything and how I felt. The session ended well. She arranged bi-weekly sessions for us so that we could see each other for two years before I graduated. It was thoughtful on her part, but it was up to me to keep the sessions.

I kept them. She was helping me discover things about myself I had no idea about before. I understood myself and didn't hate myself like before. I began to participate in different things at the university, and I found I had quite some talent for singing, though an untrained voice. Every session was a breakthrough for us, and she took every single one seriously as I progressed. The therapist often asked me about my progress in school. I told her: my grades had picked up, my health was generally good, and life was just beautiful. Then she would give me this smile, one that made me glad I'd told her that bit of inconsequential information. In our last session, before I graduated, she told me I had to face my parents and make peace with them if I wanted to forgive them. I rebelled against the idea, but she insisted. She'd seen me come so far, and she believed this was the last thing she needed me to do, and then I'd be done. I'd be free. So, I called them and spoke to them. My parents hadn't had my number for years, so they didn't recognize my voice. Each of them was filled with joy when they realized it was me, as they were still divorced. I explained to them that I forgave them for everything that happened when I was a child, but they didn't understand and just kept expressing their joy and how much they'd missed me. I tried to just be okay with that, but deep down, I was still upset. One of the things I did to cope with my pain was to sing. Singing ran in my family, and I was happy the gift fell on me because I truly love singing. I remember when I entered this singing contest. I was ready to show the world what I was made of. Surprisingly, I came in third place in the singing contest and was thrilled with myself. A boy that was hanging on to a thread of life two years ago, with no belief in life or himself, was standing there with a medal. I'd never carried one in my life.

With determination, I graduated as one of the happiest people on the planet. I believe I have a long way to go. God isn't done with me. After graduation, I connected with some people who gave me the opportunity to record an album. Recently, I have been getting more opportunities, and currently singing back up for a well-known artist. I've had the opportunity to travel the world and encourage people through music. I often think about what I would have missed had I taken my own life. I understand now that the pain I had to endure was just to help lead me to my destiny. Had my parents never left me, I would've never discovered my voice, and I wouldn't be able to do what I love to do each day. I am reminded of a song

that we used to sing:

"Why should I feel discouraged
Why should the shadows come
Why should my heart feel lonely
And long for heaven and home

When Jesus is my portion
A constant friend is He
His eye is on the sparrow
And I know He watches over me
His eye is on the sparrow
And I know He watches me"

Singing is what helped me endure my hurt and help fulfill my destiny.

Today I encourage you to find what you are passionate about and use it to

help you fight through the troubles of this world. Remember, God has His

eye on you. God Bless.

A Mother's Pain

My sons' father left me, ending a five-year relationship after discovering I was pregnant. I was a mess. It was as if somebody had pulled a chair out from underneath me, and I was falling into a bottomless abyss. I was flailing, disoriented, and depressed for so long. This man had been my strength and support even though we had our quarrels. I never thought he would walk out over something as trivial as this. "I don't want to be a father," are the last words I remember him echoing in my ear. I mean, we were only 24 at the time, so I can't say that I blame him. However, I am not excusing him either. For five years, we had been having unprotected sex. I was on "the pill" and was sure that I was protected. I wanted to do whatever it took to please and keep my man. We started out as close friends in high school, which eventually turned into a relationship following graduation. I was pretty sure I was very much in love with this man.

We attended the same college; both graduated within four years and were set to start our lives together. I got a job as an accountant for the city, and he worked as a sales manager for a large company. We talked about marriage and moving in together, but I believe he only told me those things to keep me on a leash. He knew I wanted to settle down and have a family.

Even at such a young age, I knew that I was ready. However, I can't say the same for Terry. I remember after taking three pregnancy tests and getting confirmation from my doctor, I most definitely was pregnant. I went home and cried tears of joy. I was so sure we were going to get married and have a beautiful baby. To my surprise, however, Terry did not respond the way I expected. Instead, he had news of his own. He had been promoted to General Manager and was being relocated to an out of state position. He explained that this was not the right time to have a baby. He said he was focused on his career, and I should be focusing on mine.

I convinced myself he just needed an excuse to leave, but this was too much, too confusing for me. I had no option but to be on my own. Luckily, he left the house for me. He never came back, though. I carried the pregnancy to full term and gave birth to two beautiful boys. They had their father's sparkling eyes and small nose, but my greatest pride was their flawless skin. It was chocolate, just like mine. It may sound cheesy, but that's how I knew they were my children. I raised these boys with the pride and joy any mother would. I told myself they were my sons, and I wouldn't allow them to grow up to be people who would walk out like their father (who I was still making excuses for up until then).

I did as I promised, and my boys became the sweetest, politest, and most handsome twins anyone ever saw. Strangers I randomly introduced them to on the street would say, "Aren't they beautiful?" and I would happily reply, "You know, they have my skin. Can you see it?" I probably sounded like a creep, but no one can resist two beautiful baby boys just struggling to string words together. "Goop moreeeeen." That one melted all of them. Baby talk for "good morning." I put them through school on my meager salary, and sometimes it was hardly enough for us to eat. However, I didn't mind going hungry if my sons were attending school and learning. I didn't like to ask for help. One winter, I found myself jobless after the city started scaling back. I was now living off unemployment and food stamps. We were forced to move to a more affordable place in the projects.

While this was a tough time for me, my boys were just so happy. All they knew was that mommy loved them, and where we lived was full of little boys that looked like them. That year, during Christmas, I was sure my boys would not be able to get anything since I could barely make ends meet. To my surprise, one day, a friend called me out of the blue and said he wanted to send me something. He said that God placed it on his heart to reach out. He was kind enough to send me a check that covered my bills, and I was able to purchase new bikes for my boys for Christmas. As a mother, I learned to pray for my sons. This time, I know that God answered my prayers.

I learned to give myself grace as a mother. I was never perfect, and as a new and young mom, I made mistakes after mistakes. However, one thing I know I did well was to show my children daily how to work hard, treat people fairly, and pray. In the most difficult times, I found that my relationship with God was most important and that he would bring me and my sons to better days. Eventually, God gave me an even better job, and we were able to buy a small home in the country. We didn't have much, but we always had each other. My sons and I grew closer and closer every day as they matured. I would spend hours in their room on my off days talking baby talk with them at first as if I had nothing else to do. I took them grocery shopping and to work sometimes. They were generally excited to go anywhere with me. They were surprisingly very well-behaved, and occasionally, they would hug each leg and tug at my clothes. This was one of the happiest moments of my life. Those hugs made every tear and every long night worth it all.

As they grew, they became more outspoken and did well socially and academically. I got weekly reports that they were natural spokesmen in their respective classes, connecting well with the rest of the students and gaining their trust enough to speak for them. I didn't need these reports, though; they would come back and share everything with me after a long day. I looked forward to hearing each of their stories every day. It seemed as if one day, out of the blue, they seemed to just grow up on me.

One day they were drawing on my walls and crying for me to pick them up. The next day they were taking longer in the restroom, asking for cologne, and writing little girls love notes. I do not think my heart was ready for that. I guessed I would always see them as my little baby boys. Around the age of 15, we drifted apart in some ways but were even closer in so many others. They picked up many things around the house, cleaned their rooms, and started cooking for me without me asking. They were taking accountability for being the men in the house. Momma was even able to go on one or two dates. The thing that bothered me most, I guess, was my sons didn't share as much as they used to. I guess it was to be expected. They were growing up. Their momma could no longer be their best friend, I thought to myself. I know I didn't share as much either when I hit adolescence.

I didn't support some of the friends they moved with, but I didn't take it to be much of a concern. I figured they would eventually grow out of any negative relationships as they matured. I wanted them to be able to make decisions on their own. Even though I gave my opinion, I was not too pushy. I always told them they would have to learn to navigate life for themselves. I wanted to teach them how to be independent. For the most part, all seemed to be going well. They were making good grades and had cute little girlfriends. My dad managed to put together a couple bucks and bought them a car. At this point, they were living the good life. Finally, senior year arrived, and we were all excited about the things to come— senior portraits, prom, and, most importantly, graduation. The twins both made plans to join the air force. I was so very proud of them. Then, it happened. I will never forget the day or the time: July 27th at 4:15 pm.

My sons and I were headed back from the grocery store. My boys helped me get groceries in the house like they always did. Afterward, they told me they were headed out to play some basketball at the local park. What was just a normal Saturday evening in my household turned out to be a nightmare. I remember Tee, the youngest of the twins, racing home to get me with tears in his eyes and frantic as I had ever seen. He begged me to come with him to the hospital. As we were racing to the hospital, he tried to explain to me that his brother Dee had gotten into an argument over a basketball game. They thought the dust had settled and began preparing to leave when the person Dee argued with went and got his gun from the trunk. Shots rang out at the court, hitting four bystanders and my son Dee. Bystanders called 911, and all the victims were taken to the local hospital. We rushed to the hospital, hoping to see my son, Tee's twin. When we arrived, we were met by a host of people who were at the basketball court and police officers. I screamed, "Where is my son! I want to see my son!" I remember the horrific look on my next-door neighbor's face as she had gotten to the hospital shortly before. She calmly hugged me and uttered words I will never forget, "He's gone."

This had to be a dream. I broke down into tears, and I screamed and cried. I cried and screamed. This could not be true. How could this happen? Because my pastor was the Chaplain at the hospital, I was able to see my son earlier than expected. I remember looking at his body lying there, still and lifeless. All I could do was tell him I was sorry. The police questioned my other son and everyone that was at the park. A suspect would be found and arrested as soon as possible. They would be charged with the murder of 1 and attempted murder of 3, as all the other victims survived.

At Dee's funeral, I was a shadow draped in black, tears streaming out of my eyes the entire service. I refused to say goodbye or listen to a eulogy. I just wanted to see him enter the ground in peace—my beautiful boy. As my other son drove me home, we were both quiet until he said, "Mom, I'm so sorry." I didn't truly understand why he was apologetic. I mean, this was his twin brother. He was dealing with it too. When we arrived home, two cop cars were parked at our front door. They quickly lifted their guns and pointed them at the vehicle. I was angry! Why would they be at my home after I had just buried my child? I reached to open my door and yelled at them. My son told me to calm down since he was the one they wanted, not me. I started crying and saying, "No, don't go. I need you." He stepped out and was handcuffed and taken away.

I later found out he was involved in taking the life of the young man who had taken his brother's life. Out of anger and redemption, my son Tee was now arrested for murder. The judge ended up giving my son a 30-year sentence. Tee was not in a good place mentally, and during his first year in prison, he hung himself. I lost one son to a pointless murder, and now just before their 18th birthday, I lost another to suicide. I was at the lowest point in my life. Nothing that happened up until that point could even begin to scratch the surface of the pain I experienced losing two sons. I had no reason to live anymore. I didn't know what to make of all of it. I still don't know what to make of it now. All of my support was taken from me, and I had nowhere to lean. No support, no shoulder. I cried, and I'd been crying for a long time. I stopped taking care of myself. I lost about 50 pounds, and all of my hair started falling out. I was diagnosed with depression and spent several months in a facility because the pain caused me to develop a drinking problem. For the next two years, I think I spent every night or every other night getting drunk. I even got high a few times…anything to ease my pain. After a few months in rehab, I decided I would try something different. The drugs and alcohol were not filling my void. They were only making things worse.

I decided to try going to church after a while, and it has lessened the pain. I found a community within that's very helpful, constantly checking up on me and sending thoughtful gifts. They taught me that I can lean on God whenever I need to, as He's a never-ending support and will always be there in my time of need. Whenever I call on Him, He answers. There is this Bible text I like, Isaiah 41:10: "So do not fear, for I am with you; do not be dismayed, for I am your God. I will strengthen you and help you; I will uphold you with my righteous right hand."

Though I've lost a lot, I'm learning to lean on God again, and as I get to understand Him, I am smiling a little more every day. I'm sorry if you read my story and were expecting a fairy tale ending. That's not the case here. I'm still dealing with my pain, but progress, not perfection. Some days are better than others. I do not understand God's will, but I am learning every day to accept it. It's not easy, and yes, I mourn for my boys daily. Each birthday, Christmas, and Thanksgiving are hard. I can't help but remember how excited they would be at 4 am, ready to open their gifts or sitting at the table waiting on my famous mac-n-cheese. I think about how I will never get to see them in a prom picture or cap and gown. I will never get to see them serve their country in the air force uniform. These are things that I often think about, and sometimes I shed a tear or two hundred.

One thing I have found that has helped is doing yoga. I participate in yoga three times a week. It has helped me lose the weight I gained and helped relieve the stress I feel from day to day. I went back to school and got my Master of Arts in Counseling. I have since pursued my doctorate in counseling. I am using my pain to help others get through theirs. I can honestly relate to the phrase, "Hurt by My Destiny." Each day I try to walk into my destiny. I got married and have two bonus daughters. I have my own practice, and I'm serving others. However, I still carry the pain of losing my twin boys. I leave any one of you who may be going through hard times with a few words from my favorite poem by Langston Hughes.

<u>Still Here</u>

Langston Hughes

I been scarred and battered.
My hopes the wind done scattered.
Snow has friz me,
Sun has baked me,

Looks like between 'em they done
Tried to make me

Stop laughin', stop lovin', stop livin'--
But I don't care!
I'm still here!

Bearing the Unbearable

My name is Amber, an educator from Chicago, Illinois. I lost my son to suicide when he was only 15 years old. Because of the hurt and shame that I felt, I relocated to Birmingham, Alabama. My intention was not to run away from my problems but to get away from all the people who were responsible for my son's death. I wanted to get a fresh start where no one knew me and hopefully find some type of closure for the pain I was dealing with. One Saturday afternoon, I loaded all I could in my Chevy Traverse, and I drove nearly 11 hours to what is now my home in Jefferson County, Alabama.

Giving birth to my son was one of the most joyous and memorable times of my life. I remember it as though it were yesterday. I was sitting at home, and at 9:35 am, my water broke. What was I supposed to do? I was by myself and nearly about to give birth to my baby boy right in my apartment living room. I called my brother, and he rushed home from work. My brother got me to the hospital just in time. (I'm pretty sure we broke every traffic law there was.) After a few short hours of treacherous pain, I held the most precious gift God had ever given me in my hands, my sweet Anthony. He came out with a head full of hair, which may explain all the heartburn I experienced during my pregnancy. Anthony James (AJ) was an amazing boy. He had beautiful red hair, piercing hazel eyes that changed from green to blue, and a quirky sense of humor. He loved animals, road trips, Minecraft, Legos, and chocolate ice cream. He was my sweet baby and precious angel on Earth, and now because of such hatred, he is my angel in Heaven.

Most family and friends called AJ by his middle name, which was Tyler. It was a family name. My grandfather and my father were both named Tyler. I often called him "my baby" even after he reached the age where he felt he was too old to be called that. He was born in May of 2003, was six weeks early, and weighed only 4.52 lbs. He spent 15 days in the NICU before being able to come home. While in the hospital, he spent two weeks on oxygen and was fed through a tube. Tyler had several developmental problems. For the most part, he was very "normal" and intelligent but still always just a little different from most of the other kids.

In second grade, the teasing began. He was picked on because of his hair, his glasses, and the fact that he was smaller than most of the other boys. He was seen as weak and became a target. As Tyler got older, he often wondered why people were so mean to him. He would ask me, "Mom, why can't people just be nice?" I never really knew how to answer that question, so I tried to encourage him to be the nice one. I also told him all the things a parent tells a child—that he was special, that he was smart, that he was loved. But as kids grow older, the words of a parent begin to pale in comparison to the words of their peers. In November 2013, Tyler began to show signs of depression and speak of suicide. For years, he had been tormented by several boys at his school. Tyler started saying that his father and I would be better off without him and that he didn't want to be with us anymore. At first, we thought he was just overreacting, but when the comments didn't stop, I knew he was in trouble. I knew I had to do something, so I took him to the local emergency room. Sadly, this particular ER didn't really deal with mental health issues, and we were referred to a therapist. He soon began weekly therapy and seemed to be feeling better. But this was short-lived.

In the summer of 2015, I got a new teaching job in a better school district, but this meant Tyler would have to change schools. I helped him see that this was a new beginning and that the bullies from his previous school would be a thing of the past; he was nervous but still excited. As he started 7th grade at his new school, he met one boy with whom he had common interests, and they became friends. However, the teasing and bullying continued at this school too. Tyler was an easy target because he didn't like what other kids liked. He didn't play sports; he loved Dr. Who, YouTube, and anime and would rather read a book than play outside. He was soon being called a "loser" or a "geek." He was devastated. The difference was that he stopped telling me about the bullying. He felt that I was going to overreact and make a big deal about things. He was correct. I was going to do everything in my power to protect my baby. What mother wouldn't? When I began to do more investigation, I learned that Tyler had reported several incidents to his teachers and principals. The principal told him to just avoid the other boy. I asked Tyler why he hadn't told me this was going on, and he said, "Mom, you can't fix this." What was I supposed to do? I was completely lost at this point. How could so much have happened, and those who were supposed to protect him did nothing to keep my child safe. I did not receive anything, not even so much as an email or phone call to let me know what was going on. There was no way I was having that or letting any of it slide.

I made an appointment with the administration of the school, and as my brother would say, "I showed my ass." I was so upset and cursed that principal from here to there. I know this was not the proper way to handle this situation, but I did not know what else to do. How could they allow this to go on in their school when they were completely aware and STILL did absolutely nothing. Well, let's just say that I left that school (with the help of security) more upset than I have ever been in my life. I'm glad I did not own a firearm because I probably would have used it that day. I contacted the board of education, but of course, they did nothing as well. I felt helpless at this point. All I could do was cry. My son was under constant attack, and no one seemed to care but me. However, I wasn't giving up that easily. After I raised a little more hell, the kid who was the main bully was expelled from school. I guess the administration did not want me calling the local news stations and protesting outside the school, as I told them I would. Nonetheless, I made the decision to withdraw Tyler from school. I decided I was going to home-school him. This was the only way I thought I could protect my baby. However, being a single parent and trying to be the provider did not work out as well as I had planned.

Tyler was often at home alone and was suffering from something known as cyberbullying. It seems the kid who was kicked out of school was upset, and so were his family and friends. Prior to being expelled, he was a star football and basketball player who had high hopes for a prosperous future. Because of his strong support in the community, people turned on AJ. So many people were making posts on social media about how my son was a punk and how they were going to beat him up whenever they saw him. For nearly two years, this was going on, and I had no idea. I wanted to give my son space without overcrowding, but as I was cleaning up one day, I decided to check his computer, and this was how I found this horrific information.

At this point, I was in complete rage. I wanted to drive to each one of their homes and beat the life out of them. Why are you messing with my baby is all I could think? He would never hurt a fly, and now you're upset because he exposed a bully. I took Tyler to my dad's home, which was about 30 minutes away. I felt he needed some fresh air, and I did not want him to see me overacting, as he had already predicted that I would. Tyler stayed with his grandparents for about a week. When I felt he was ready, I went to get him over the weekend. I thought for sure everything was okay, at least for the most part. On our way home, he was very talkative; he did not really talk about how he felt, just that he had a great time with grandpa and that he was hungry. We stopped for some burgers and milkshakes, and we headed home. It seemed to be going all too well. After we got home, Tyler went into his room, typical of teenage boys. I thought he just needed some time alone. After about 30 minutes, I went to check on him, and that's when I found him. He had taken an extremely large amount of pain pills he had stolen from CVS pharmacy when he was with his granddad. There was no warning and no note. Nothing.

After a frantic call to 911 and 25 minutes of CPR by paramedics, Tyler was transported to the local hospital and then taken by helicopter to Children's Hospital. The doctors did everything they could to pump the medicine out of his system. However, everything they did failed. All the medicine had ruined his already weak system. On October 13, 2018, at 10:32 in the dark night, Tyler was pronounced dead. What was actually a good day turned into the worst day of my life. After his death, I was numb. I don't really remember a lot of the next few weeks. I remember just sitting in the dark and crying for several hours each day. My father came to stay with me for a while. Honestly, I blamed him for allowing Tyler to steal the pills though I knew in my heart it really was not his fault. I was just mad at the world. I was mad at God. I was mad at my family. I was extremely mad at the bullies who had tormented my baby.

I'm not really a religious person, but I encountered an old man one day as I was during my morning run. If I were religious, I would probably say he was my guardian angel. He was sitting on the park bench as I ran by. I noticed him there almost every morning as I ran, but this particular morning it was something different about him. He asked me for some cash. I had watched him day after day being passed over by others who just ignored him. Normally, I do not carry cash, but on this particular day, I had five dollars in my pocket because I was going to get a hot coffee after my morning run. I reached in to give the old man the five bucks, and he touched my hand and mumbled, "Teach the others to be kind." It was then that I realized that as educators, parents, and people in general, we have done our children a disservice. We've taught them about bullies and bullying behavior. We've given them detailed ideas of what bullies do and told them not to be one. What we haven't done, though, is teach them how to be nice to one another. We just assume they know. We hope that when we tell them to "be nice," they know how, but often they don't.

I knew I had to do something. That is when my non-profit organization was born. I started it as a Facebook page with the intent of sharing stories of kindness and reminders to be kind to one another, even when it wasn't easy. This also led to starting a Weekly Kindness Challenge that gave people a kindness task to perform each week. At first, there were only a few hundred followers. Soon after, I was asked to speak at schools where I shared Tyler's story. Then, I started speaking at other schools, sharing Tyler's story and using participation activities to show kids the real power of their words and the power of kindness. To date, we have donated thousands of dollars, gifts, toys, and shoes to help those in need. We have sponsored several workshops, events, and even a huge gala, where the mayor of the city announced that October 13 would always be Anthony's day. To date, we have given presentations in at least 20 schools across Alabama and Illinois, and our Facebook family has grown to over 8000. It is my deepest hope that we can change the culture of our society and leave all of the negativity and name-calling behind. Creating a culture of kindness has to start with one person, so why not with me?

I'm sorry if you were looking for some very storybook ending or how my life has been great since I found Christ. That's not my story. I am still hurting every day as I struggle to raise my other two kids. I am not a perfect mother by any means, but I am trying my best. I use my foundation as a way to bring happiness to my hurt soul. I still feel the hurt each day and want to just see my son again. This is a pain that I am not sure I will ever get over, but I try my best each day to make him proud by being kind to someone else. I challenge you to be kind each day as well.

The Bad Apple

Growing up, the one thing I heard the most was, "You'll never be anything." I didn't blame them, though. I was the bad apple. I got into a lot of unnecessary trouble. I would say that I was looking for attention or maybe a sense of belonging. When I was eight years old, my mother died from cancer, and my father abandoned me. For years, I was angry at his decision to leave me to be raised by a complete stranger. In grade school, I immediately started getting into trouble. It started with small, petty things such as talking about other kids, trying to be the class clown, and eventually carried into stealing. Stealing eventually led to fighting. When I was in middle school, I got into a lot of fights. I spent most of my Jr. High school years in alternative school and in school suspension. When my father left, a foster family named the Smiths took me in. They were nice people, and they tried their best to do right by me, but they were not my parents. Whatever they tried to do never seemed good enough for me.

As I matriculated through high school, I was labeled the "bad" kid. As I began my high school career, I did not get into as much trouble, but when I did, it escalated because of the name I had previously created for myself. I thought to myself, since no one cared about me, *why should I care anymore?* I started falling back into some of my old habits. I became rebellious and defiant toward my teachers. I wanted so badly to be loved and treated fairly, but I could not seem to receive that type of affection, so instead, I did things for attention. If I was going to be labeled the bad kid after trying to do better, I might as well be the bad kid in my eyes. I did just enough work not to fail my classes. Right after school, you could find me in the parking lot passing out dime bags to the rich kids who loved to get high. One time I got into a huge altercation with a fellow student. He tried to short me some money, and when I confronted him about it, he wanted to make a big scene. Naturally, I had to pay my supplier, so I wasn't going to let him short me. I had to handle him. I will never forget that day. All day I had been watching Steve. That was the redhead kid who owed me money.

When 3:00pm came, I knew that he would be walking to his new jeep his parents had bought him, and I would catch him there to get my money. Sure enough, 3:00pm came, and the bell rang. I saw Steve headed to his jeep. I snuck right up beside him and asked, "Where's my money?" He replied that he did not have it and asked what I was going to do about it. He began being very loud as to make a big scene because deep down, he was really scared. After all, at that time, I was about 6"2 250 pounds of muscle. At that moment, I smacked him across the head. One blow to the head and he was lying on the ground unconscious. That was a big mistake. Steven was the son of Richard and Michele, who were the local farmers that owned that town. They had nearly everyone in that town in their back pocket. That one second of what I called handling my business caused me what seemed to be a lifetime of pain.

I was arrested and thrown into juvenile detention center. Here I was, 16 years old at the time, going back and forth to court, not knowing if I would ever see daylight again. Luckily, the Smiths were able to get me a good lawyer. Also, my mom worked for the Judge before she died, and he took it easy on me. I was given three years of probation and had to finish my sophomore year in alternative school. When fall came of my Jr year, I decided I wanted to play football. The coach had convinced me to play. At this point, what did I have to lose? I hadn't played since I was a young kid, but I had the body for it. Midway through my junior year, I was dominating the football field. I felt that was the only place I could release all my frustrations. By my senior year, I had over ten schools that had interest in me. I thought maybe I could make something of myself and get away from all my troubles. It turned out that nobody wanted the troublemaker on their team. Several coaches came to see me, they loved my size, athletic ability, and tape, but when asked what type of kid I was, most teachers said I was a problem. For the life of me, I could not understand how the people who had pledged to support and help me reach my goals and dreams were the same ones keeping me from reaching goals and dreams. I understand that I had gotten into several fights and I had a bad reputation, but I felt mainly misunderstood and abandoned. Nobody ever seemed concerned about why I acted the way I did. No one ever tried to get to the root cause of my problems. It felt as if I were damaged goods and no one cared. Not to mention, not once did I get in trouble in my junior and senior years of high school. I couldn't get in trouble. My probation officer was going to lock me up if I did.

With my previous record and lack of support from teachers, I was unable to receive a scholarship to play football. I was really crushed. I felt if given the proper chance, I could have progressed to college to become one of the greats. I didn't go to college immediately after high school, and I wasn't working. Subsequently, I found myself back into the drug dealing life. It was the only thing I knew. The drug dealing business appears glamorous, but it's not what they make it out to be in the movies. I got into a lot of altercations, and I constantly had to watch my back. My foster parents' house got shot up more than one time. (Besides being an adult, my foster parents adopted me and allowed me to stay with them). My life went on and on like that as I grew older. My parents threatened to kick me out of the house, but I didn't believe they would do it. I got into trouble a few more times and reached home to see my things packed neatly outside the gate. I banged on the door for almost 30 minutes, refusing to accept it, but nobody answered the door. I saw the curtain rustling sometimes and knew they were in, but still, there was no response. So, I carried my belongings and left.

I stayed at a friend's house for the time being, and during this time, I turned worse. Everything I had been doing while in my parents' house was magnified now. I now brought different women into the house every night. My friends hailed me every time, and it got into my head. I even became so careless as not to use a condom and whisper in the girl's ears to please use a pill. I rode on the assumption that no lady wanted the burden of a baby from a street guy. However, there was this girl that kept joking about it when I mentioned it to her. I dismissed her as unserious then, but my friends huddled up with me and told me I should take a woman seriously if she even talked about it. I ignored them, saying they were paranoid, and besides, it was a one-night stand. How would I ever find her? Six months later, this lady showed up pregnant at my friend's door and said she was looking for me. I was lost and appalled, and she dragged me outside. She explained that she had been taking the pill and hurting her body, so she had stopped for a while. I was so confused. "So, the solution was to have a baby?" I asked her. She simply shrugged. She said she wouldn't bother me with taking care of her, but I'd have to pay child support. I told her I didn't have child support money and I was broke. Truly, I did not have the money. Yes, I was making money from slinging dope, but I was spending it fast as I got it. I didn't even have a bank account. Of course, when she gave birth to the kid, I wasn't able to pay anything. At first, she was calling and raving over the phone, but I really didn't care and always cut her off.

I was surprised when the police broke down my friend's door and grabbed me one day. They took me to the station and showed me a baby picture, and asked why I wasn't paying child support. Did I want him to die? I tried to explain the situation to them, but they threw me in a cell and told me I wouldn't be coming out until I paid three months' worth of child support. I was in the cell for two weeks until they came to release me one day. My parents had paid for it. I was so grateful and tried to hug them, but they were unamused. They told me the only condition they were helping me on was that I'd go to the military. I resisted at first, but they threatened to withdraw the money from the police. So, I reluctantly agreed. I joined the air force at age 22.

The military tested and stretched me to the limit. I was barely surviving at first, but I pulled through eventually. Everything there gave me a different perspective on life. While I was there, a fellow student introduced me to the teachings of Buddhism. It completely changed my life. When I came out of basic training, I was a changed man. The things that used to excite me no longer did. Buddhism is all about discovering inner peace. The peace and joy that I had been missing, I was now able to find through the teaching of the 4 Noble Truths. One thing studying Buddhism gave me was the power to forgive my parents. I know this sounds selfish, especially since my mother passed away, but I had to learn to forgive. I was angry at her for leaving me. I carried that weight for so long. Also, I had to forgive my dad. He was a coward and afraid to teach me how to be a man. Nonetheless, I learned he was just a kid, and he was probably scared of taking on such responsibilities. After having my own child, I understood how hard it was, so I learned to forgive him. Once I got myself together, I was determined to be a better father than he was.

After completing the basic training, I was assigned to Montgomery, AL. I began taking online courses. With hard work and dedication, I obtained my bachelor's and master's degree in Computer Science. You should have seen the look on my parents' faces at both graduations. My foster dad shared a few tears of joy. With the completion of my college degrees, I was able to move up through the ranks in the military. What started out as just a deal with my parents eventually became a lifestyle that I loved. I was able to travel the world and see places I never would have seen selling dope in Birmingham.

I moved up through the ranks of the air force and eventually became a master sergeant. I regularly talked to the soldiers about practicing Buddhism, and even though most of them laughed at me, the peace I experienced was amazing, and many noted the change I made. I tried reconnecting with my baby girl. I strived to be a better father and a better man each day. I'm trying to right some of the wrongs I made in my past life. My baby mother and I are constantly striving to co-parent; she even took me off child support because I stepped up to the plate and started taking care of my child. Even though we disagree and argue like anyone else, we are determined to work through everything and be the best parents we can be for our baby girl.

Presently, I volunteer at the YMCA as a football and basketball coach. I use this opportunity to pour into young males like myself who may be struggling for some direction and need someone to look up to. I try my best to help them appreciate their greatness and potential. I even reached out to my real father. We are trying to develop a relationship, but it's rocky. Nonetheless, I'm going to keep on trying. I honestly don't have some fairy tale ending. I don't have some big shebang or any great advice. My story is still being written each day. I'm just learning to grow, seek the truth and find my inner peace.

Hurt by My Destiny: What does it all mean?

I bet you are wondering, "What do all these different stories have to do with me?" Maybe you saw yourself in the book; maybe you did not. One thing is for certain, and two for sure; we all have our own battles to fight. Sometimes in the midst of those battles, we find ourselves in a well of hurt. For some, this hurt could be physical or mental. For others, the pain could be financial, psychological, or spiritual. No matter what the case, my brothers and sisters, you are not alone in your fight. Life is but a cycle, and everything that may seem unbearable to you has already been conquered by someone else. Someone has already overcome the same situation you are dealing with. As Kirk Franklin would say, your pain was preparation for your destiny. Pain is only a small ingredient that goes into your destiny's recipe.

Personally, I don't like raw eggs, flour, or even cooking oil alone, but these ingredients, when mixed together, are all used to make cake, and I love cake. I understand that in order to get the thing I love, I have to mix some things in the recipe that I don't really love. That's how life is sometimes. You get a mixture of hurt, pain, failure, defeat, victory, triumph, and success, and it all makes one great recipe called destiny. Your trials can be a testimony for someone else.

My prayer is that this book has blessed you or encouraged you in one way or the other. I hope it makes you realize your pain is only temporary, and it's only there to help you get to your destiny. Your disappointments are needed to get you to the place God has strategically ordained you to be. Godspeed to you all!

No Hurt, No Healing
Know Hurt, Know Healing
Fight Despair,
Fulfill Destiny

Hurt by My Destiny

Bibliography

Guest, Edgar Albert. "See It Through by Edgar Albert Guest | Poetry Foudation." *Poetry Foundation*, 2022 Poetry Foundation, 13 Apr. 2021, https://www.poetryfoundation.org/poems/44318/see-it-through.

Published, Independently. *Holy Bible King James Version Including the Apocrypha and the Book of Enoch*. 2017.

"His Eye Is on the Sparrow." Hymnary.org, 2011 hymnary.org/text/why_should_I-feel_discouraged

"Still Here by Langston Hughes." *Hello Poetry*, 2020, hellopoetry.com/poem/348/still-here/.

Tartakovsky, Margarita. "Healthy Ways to Navigate Grief." *Psych Central*, Psych Central, 7 Nov. 2013, https://psychcentral.com/blog/healthy-ways-to-navigate-grief#1.

Made in the USA
Columbia, SC
13 March 2023

13459943R00090